Chippenham Street Names

CHRIS DALLIMORE

Copyright © 2018 Chris Dallimore

All rights reserved.

ISBN: 978-0-244-13344-3

CONTENTS

1	Introduction	Pg 5
2	Town Centre	Pg 10
3	Over the Bridge	Pg 40
4	London Road	Pg 53
5	Monkton Park	Pg 61
6	Langley and Greenways	Pg 68
7	Hardenhuish	Pg 79
8	Woodlands and Audley	Pg 91
9	Lowden and Rowden	Pg 100
10	Hungerdown and Ladyfield	Pg 109
11	Queens Crescent and Cepen Park South	Pg 116
12	Allington and Cepen Park North	Pg 121
13	Frogwell and Derriads	Pg 126
14	Pewsham	Pg 136
	Conclusion	Pg 157
	Acknowledgments	Pg 158
	Bibliography	Pg 159

1 - Introduction

'The historical association of Chippenham should be perpetuated in the naming of new streets' - Edward Newall Tuck, 1937.

This book should be of interest to anyone with links to the market town of Chippenham in Wiltshire. Its aim is to appeal to as wide an audience as possible, so even if the history of the whole town is not of particular interest, a current or former resident can at least find out more about their own street.

The High Street, c1904.

In most cases, only residential streets or those which previously were so, such as Foundry Lane and River Street, are included. Many photographs you will see here are from private collections which have not been available to the public before, but collaboration on social media has allowed them to be shared for the first time. With the assistance of current and former residents of the town, official records, newspapers and many other sources, it has been possible to explain why particular names were chosen. Any challenges to errors or omissions are welcome, as although the aim is to cover every street and be 100% accurate, this may not always have been possible. It must be remembered that much of the available historical information was written by earlier historians, or passed on by word of mouth. Neither sources are entirely reliable, and further research may be required for a more definitive history of a particular street of interest.

Work starts on Emery Gate, c1985. Photograph - Tim Gatherum.

Some street names have changed over the years or have disappeared with the roads themselves. Many origins of the old street names have long been lost, though they were recorded on maps or in books, their meanings have not always been remembered. It is often possible to make reasonable assumptions to decide why a particular name was chosen.

Streets are often named after what was present before, and evidence of this can be found through consultation of old maps or land ownership records. Descriptive elements of the environment, such as nature or geographical features, may also have been chosen. Field names are commonly used, acting as a kind of memorial to the countryside that has been built over, and it is often the most obvious choice. Names ending in 'mead' or 'leaze' can denote the former existence of a meadow or pasture, and 'close' may indicate land that had been enclosed or set aside for a particular purpose.

Other streets are named after notable residents deemed worthy of the honour by those in authority. These may be politicians, educators, businessmen, or philanthropists, though often the significance of their contribution is lost over time.

Love & Sons during WW1. Photograph - Ann Brinkworth.

Like other towns, Chippenham willingly sacrificed the lives of many of its young men during the two world wars. The majority of these are commemorated on a memorial either in the Market Place or in one of the churches. Some of these were also chosen to be remembered through street names on the Pewsham housing estate.

The first name we should concern ourselves with, is the name of Chippenham itself. There are two schools of thought regarding the origin of the name; the first was that it was named after an individual called *Cepen* or *Cyppa*, and the second is that derives from *chepyng* and *ham*, which together forms a Saxon phrase meaning 'market-village'.

The first theory is supported by early examples of the use of *Cepen* on coins minted in Chippenham during the reign of Ethelred II 978-1015.[1] Also, Chippenham is listed as *Cepen* in the Domesday book of 1086, with a population of an estimated c600.

The second theory is supported by the Saxon words; *ceap*, which means goods that are bought and sold, or *chepyng*, meaning 'market' (a word which was in use long after Saxon times),

---

[1] Platts, Arnold, (1947), p.2

combined with *ham,* which was Saxon for a 'house-farm' or 'village' (similar to hamlet). Therefore 'Chepyng-ham' would result in a Saxon word for 'market-village'.

Local pronunciation is often an important factor in the evolution of place names. The antiquarian John Britton wrote on the people of Chippenham; - 'the lower class, though they speak an imperfect dialect, deliver themselves in as good English than those of any town in the west of England'. Nevertheless, the local accent would have influenced how the name was recorded, up until relatively recent times when general literacy had improved. Later, Jackson discusses the use of what he calls 'railway pronunciation', when just two syllables are used to say 'Chip-nam', but fortunately by this time, record keeping was sufficient enough to preserve the spelling that we use today.[2]

Chippenham has always been a commuter town. A Roman Road ran to the south of Chippenham from Bath to Mildenhall, passing close to the small settlement of *Verlucio* at Sandy Lane. This was gradually superseded by the coach road from Bath to London, which spawned numerous coaching inns and hostelries in Chippenham, which were required to cater for travellers. Later this would be replaced by the A4, with a much changed route taking in all main settlements.

The Wiltshire & Berkshire Canal had an arm that entered Chippenham, which amongst other produce, delivered coal from the coalfields at Camerton.

A huge leap in connectivity with the rest of the country, if not the world, came with the Great Western Railway that is still in use today. Only the M4 motorway, which had been originally planned to pass south of Chippenham before opening in 1971, has had a more significant impact on the growth of the town.

'God's Wonderful Railway' was completed in June 1841, using the less favoured broad gauge, which would be replaced by narrow gauge in 1892. A nine-arched viaduct that cuts through the town, known as the Western Arches, was built by Brunel using stone excavated

This was once been a common sight in Chippenham. The main line from Bristol to London has through the town since 1841.

---

[2] Jackson, J.E., (1856), pp.3-4.

7

from the Box tunnel.³ This stone was also used in the construction of the train station buildings.
The northwest side partially collapsed in 1848 when the bridge was widened to allow for another track.

In 1914, a German traveller called George Iffland arrived in Chippenham. Having been unwell for some time, things took a turn for the worse when he shot one of his travelling companions. They were at the Waverley Temperance Hotel in the Market Place when the incident took place, which ended with Iffland killing himself in the same manner. He had said to witnesses that he thought everyone he passed in London was shouting 'German!' at him, and there was a mob following him with the intent to kill. An inquest was held at the Old Road Inn which returned a verdict of 'suicide whilst in a state of unsound mind'.
What was relevant about this particular tragic incident, was that George and his party should never have even been in the town - they had meant to travel to Chippenham in *Cambridgeshire*!⁴

The Chippenham Folk Festival is held every year in May and draws a large number of visitors to the town.

Much of the expansion of the town during the 20th century has been due to the building of council houses. Originally, the system for awarding prospective tenants a house was based on factors such as employment and reliability, rather than poverty or disability.
The largest employer in the town, Westinghouse, paid the council £1,500 to reserve the right to nominate its employees ahead of others on the waiting list. Also during war time, priority was given to those working at nearby RAF Hullavington.
This problem was further compounded by the issue of 'council house cuckoos', a name given to those who could easily afford normal rented accommodation, but continued to live on the 'subsidy of fellow ratepayers'. All this was before the 'Right to Buy' scheme was introduced by the Housing Act of 1980, which further affected

---

³ Baines, Richard, (2009), p.119.

⁴ Daily Herald, 7th August 1914.

the availability of tenancies for those in the most need.[5] There were 974 council houses in Chippenham by 1950.[6]

The motor car has had a huge impact on the streets of Chippenham. With most households owning at least one vehicle, the Victorian streets are now fully lined with parked cars, drastically changing the appearance of the town.

Further changes are now taking place. More homes are in the process of construction to the north of the town and there are plans for expansion to the south and east as well.
A balance must be found between housing needs and preserving the history and character of the town.

---

[5] Wiltshire Times, 27th November 1937.

[6] Wiltshire Times, 11th March 1950.

2 - Town Centre

At the centre of Chippenham is **The Bridge**. Without it the town would not have prospered, especially as the bridge enabled the main route from Bath to London to pass across the River Avon. A bridge of some kind would have existed since the town's earliest days, though this would probably have been made from timber and would not have been able to carry the heavier forms of transportation.
In 1746, Samuel Simpson noted that 'Chippenham, commonly called "Chipnam", is a large, populous, well-built town, and has a good bridge of 16 arches over the Avon.' Back then, the bridge stretched along from the High Street to the junction with Foghamshire and Monkton Hill, the river being much wider than it is now.

Bridge Timeline

1578 - The bridge is described as having 15 arches. At this time heavy loads were kept away as bridge was unsafe, and instead used a ford further up stream.
1615 - Two arches fell into the river, meaning it could not be used again until 1641.
1684 - Teams of men were hired to break up ice around the arches of the bridge in the 'Great Ffroste', and were paid with beer for their work.
1758 - The bridge was widened.
1788 - More alterations including the rails taken down.
1796 - A substantial restoration took place. The bridge was widened by 30 feet and more arches and a 'symmetrical balustrade and parapet' was added, a small section of which exists although in a poor state of repair.
1805 - An application was made to erect a Toll Gate on the bridge.
1818 - The Toll House was first recorded as being in existence and would later be known as 'Higgins on the Bridge.'
1834 - A Gas lamp was installed.
1878 - Widening took place on the Bath Road side of the bridge to allow for a pavement to be made.
1959 - A pedestrian bridge was built next to the old bridge.
1966 - The new bridge officially opened on 2nd May.

1968 - The last serious flood took place in July, since then the risk of flood has been further prevented by various measures including flood defences.

In 1574, Queen Elizabeth rode over the Bridge on her return back to London from Bristol and crossed the river Avon by the town bridge, or by the ford at Harden's Copse, finding the experience most displeasing. The story tells, that she exclaimed; 'Oddsbodikins, these Chippenham people shall have a new bridge!' Whether this is true or not can't be proven, but her sister Mary did order funding to be made available for this purpose when she granted the town Charter in 1554.[7]

There was a turnpike house on an island on the bridge, which later became divided into two shops. The Higgins family lived there for over 40 years during the reign of Queen Victoria, and became affectionately known by locals as 'Higgins' on the bridge' even after this time.[8] Businesses which used this building up until its demolition for the new bridge included; Spinkes stationary, Higgins Ironmongers and confectionary, Buckeridge's (later Sebastian Palmer) watchmakers and Bowell's newsagent and stationers.

The town bridge before its replacement. Photograph - Robin Hardie.

The town mill used to stand alongside the bridge and originally belonged to the Rowden Manor estate until 1810, when it was passed to Esmead Edridge of the Monkton Park estate. Only a few years later in 1816, the mill was destroyed in an arson attack. Samuel Dowling and Ralph Hale Gaby were in charge of the mill, and received a letter threatening such action unless they lowered their price of flour. The mill was soon rebuilt. There is a date stone with the year '1817' inscribed on it in the possession of Gough's Solicitors, whose office is at Mill House, 1 New Road. This was the former home of the Collen's, who worked the mill from 1837 to 1948. It then became a branch of the National Westminster Bank in 1953.

After the mill closed in 1948 there was brief hope of keeping the building when the NAAFI showed an interest, but due to an

---

[7] Daniell, J.J., (1894), pp.93-94.

[8] White, George A.H., (1924), p.30.

increasing price tag given by final owners HRS Sainsbury of Trowbridge, they chose Wood Lane instead.[9]

The mill was demolished in 1957 by L Maslen & Co. Ltd of Devizes as part of a modernisation plan which included a new row of shops and eventually a new town bridge, both of which are architecturally uninspiring. Two of the mill stones were saved to be used to create a permanent memorial to the mill in Island Park, however in the end the idea was shelved and the stones buried there instead. Incredulously, a 400 year old Plane tree which was a town landmark, was cut down to make way for the rank of shops. Any chance of an opposition was prevented as it removed before the planning application had been approved. Its loss was mourned by many at the time.

Almost every town has a main road called **High Street**, and it is the most common street name in the country with over 5,000 examples. Chippenham's has changed greatly over the years, but some of its historical features can still be appreciated especially when looking above the lower floors and their modern facades.

Chippenham Town Hall takes pride of place here, but it is not the town coat of arms which stand proudly above it. The inscription underneath explains;

'The Corporation of Chippenham erected the Arms of Joseph Neeld Esq. the founder of this hall and Market Place in acknowledgement of his Public Munificence, 1851.'

The town hall was built by Neeld in 1834, and is probably his greatest legacy. Two old inns used to stand here before it was built; the Cannon and the Antelope.

Looking up the High Street from the bridge. Postcard sent in 1905.

One of the most architecturally pleasing buildings to grace the High Street, unfortunately no longer exists. Number 17 and 18 was Joe Buckles Fish and Poultry shop, a Tudor timber-framed building. Joseph Henry Buckle was born in 1873 at the Bear Hotel, where his father was landlord. He was captain of Chippenham Fire Brigade from 1914 to 1934, during a period of technological transition, moving from horse-

---

[9] Taylor, Kay S., (2015), p.59.

drawn to a petrol engine powered fire appliance. He was also involved with the setting up of the swimming club near Long Close. He regularly won local and national competitions for his window dressings.[10] In 1943, whilst she was staying at Badminton, Queen Mary visited the shop to view Buckles collection of antique firemarks. The shop was known as 'Little Harrods' by the locals and there was much sadness when it was demolished c1963, due to it falling into disrepair after Joe Buckle died. The present 'Bristol and West' building was built here later.[11]

At 22 and 23 High Street is an impressive grade II listed, four storey building which was built in a 'Mannerist Classical style' in 1908.[12] This replaced a Tudor building which was home to Blackford's Ironmongers. By the 1960s it had become the International Stores, and has been used by many popular businesses since, including SK Fruits and Stead and Simpson.

Number 24 and 25 High Street was once an 18th-century building with a 'handsome Corinthian facade' attributed to John Wood, the Elder of Bath. This facade was originally part of another 18th-century house at Bowden Hill. This address was for a while, the home of George A White who was author of *Chippenham in Bygone Days*.
The Society for the Protection of Ancient Buildings fought to save it, but in 1932 the building was demolished by Blackford's of

This elegant facade was sold in 1932 when the new Woolworths was built.

Calne, making way for a new Woolworths that opened in April 1933. The frontage was bought by Thomas Cook, the founder of Cook's Travels, taken down piece by piece, and re built for the end wall of his 'Chippenham Rooms' art gallery, at what is now Kingswood School, Sion Hill Place, Bath.[13]
Woolworths was rebuilt again in 1975. Eventually, this popular store closed in 2009 and is divided into three shops.

---

[10] Jefferies, S., (1987), p.30.

[11] Smith, C., (1977), p.25.

[12] https://www.britishlistedbuildings.co.uk

[13] Wiltshire Times & Trowbridge Advertiser, 31 December 1932.

The Co-operative Society building at the bottom of the High Street next to the bridge, was built in 1890. Used by the Co-op for about 100 years, it is now the home of Wilkinsons.

The George Hotel in the High Street is now used for shops.

Another reminder of the past, comes from closer inspection of WH Smith which was previously The George Hotel, an old coaching Inn which was known by the locals as the 'Big George'. Brunel reputedly lodged here, probably before he established a more permanent base whilst building his Great Western Railway.[14]

Two modern shopping centres branch off High Street; Emery Gate and Borough Parade. These have witnessed great change in recent times, and many popular shops have come and gone. Borough Parade was built after Sainsbury's moved to Bath Road in 1990. Before, it was occupied by the cattle market after it had moved there from the market place in 1910, staying until 1954 when it moved to Cocklebury. The street market has been resident in various locations, and is now situated in the pedestrianised High Street on Friday and Saturday of each week.

Emery Gate opened on 28 July 1986, its vehicular access coming off **Emery Lane.** Emery was the name of one of the fields here next to the river Avon. Emery Lane used to be called Chapel Row, due to the non-conformist chapels in the vicinity. There are a couple of theories on the origin of Emery. The first, is that it is a corruption of 'Hail Mary' which would have often been heard coming from the nearby Mary chapel attached to St Andrews Church. The second is that it is a corruption of 'Almonry', which is a place where alms were distributed to the poor. Emery was recorded as 'Ymbyri' in 1314, 'Emerygate' in 1592, 'Ymberry' in 1603, and 'Ymbrye' in 1664.[15]

On the right when entering Emery Lane, the first building before the supermarket is the former Tabernacle United Reformed Church. Its origins are Calvinist-Methodist, whose preachers became active in

---

[14] Griffiths, T.J., (1982),

[15] Gover, J.E.B., (1939), p.89.

the area from 1742. The first Tabernacle was built in 1770, then restored and added to in 1826.[16]

Cornelius Winter served here from 1776, as well as in Christian Malford and Castle Combe. In 1797 the Congregational and Independent Churches joined, with the Rev Clift of Chippenham, who was a student of Cornelius Winter's academy in Marlborough, one of its founder members.

In 1904, further alterations were made to accommodate an organ. Outside, facing onto Emery Lane, is a 'semi-elliptical arched carriage entrance' now blocked up and the words 'congregational church' inscribed on the edge roll.[17] Later it became the home of the United Reformed Church. The site has now been sold for non-religious use.

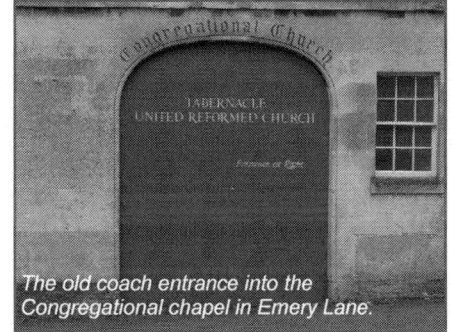

The old coach entrance into the Congregational chapel in Emery Lane.

The popularity of non-conformity in the area was largely due to the Dissenter links in the textile trade. In John Britton's *The Beauties of Wiltshire* of 1801, he noted that the people of Chippenham had a 'tendency to respect religion' and that they 'pay deference to each other's principles without yielding their own.' This would allow personal expression of beliefs without fear of persecution or ridicule.[18]

Most of the older buildings in Emery Lane were demolished in the late 1960s and turned into a car park. The Friday market moved from the bottom of **River Street** to here in 1973, making way for a Sainsbury's supermarket, which opened 7 October 1975. This store pioneered an integral freezer section, as it was the first supermarket to have one.

When Emery Gate shopping precinct was built in 1986, the Friday market had to move home again, this time to the covered area in the Bath Road car park.

---

[16] Baines, Richard, (2009), p.135.

[17] https://www.britishlistedbuildings.co.uk

[18] Baines, Richard, (2009), p.136.

River Street was originally known as Back Lane. It ran down to the river to Back Avon Bridge, a small footbridge that crossed to the Ivy Estate.

River Street. This is now Borough Parade Car Park.

There was a hive of activity in River Street. A silk factory was in operation here in 1851 employing 46 women. This was owned by John Spiers, who was originally from Bethnal Green.[19] In the 1870s, James Warrilow's gun making business took over the old silk factory building, before later moving to Foundry Lane.

Richard Slade & Sons Brewery also started here from the Woolpack Inn c1879, before also moving across town to larger premises in Union Road in 1890. In 1926, Slade's was absorbed by George's Bristol Brewery.

Public houses served those living and working in the street. The Lamb, which was at the top of the hill, existed as early as 1629 but was demolished in 1958. The George and Dragon was here in 1870. The Swan pub was further down towards the river, until it too was demolished in 1912 to enable an enlargement of the new cattle market yard. The Swan was affectionately known as 'Paddy's Goose' by the locals.[20] It roughly stood on the corner of where Sainsbury's used to be before the building, later Discount World, was also demolished in 1996. Sainsbury's relocated to Bath Road in 1990.

The remaining properties in River Street were demolished in 1973, and all that is left now is a small pedestrian access point to the Borough Parade car park. The Christian Bookshop, which closed in January 2018, is the only property still surviving.

Just off the High Street, leading to Emery Lane, is **Chapel Lane**. This is named after the Baptist chapel, set up by Thomas Shuttleworth, which opened here on 10 June 1804.[21] Built by Paul Porter of Bath, at least one hundred people attended the opening ceremony, at which five parishioners were taken to be baptised in

---

[19] 1851 Census

[20] Platts, Arnold, (1947), p.71.

[21] Baines, Richard, (2009), p.135.

the river at Westmead. A baptistery was added in 1818 for use in the winter.

The street has had many names over time, including 'Inchels Place', 'Marshalls Place' and 'Gutter Lane'.

The change from Gutter Lane to Chapel Lane took place in July 1953, when the Deacon of the chapel requested it. The town council agreed, but there was strong opposition from some of the councillors. Their main concerns were who would pay, and should a name which used for many years, be lost. No evidence was found that the name was of any historical significance, and it would not have been the first time an old name was changed, an earlier example being that of Blind Lane to Gladstone Road.[22]

The Old Baptist Chapel in Chapel Lane was built in 1804.

Mr Wilson's Grammar School was originally in St Mary Street but moved to Gutter Lane. This shut it 1900 after the council bought the building and school for £10, and was later used as a storage for Messrs Hulbert, Light & co. This private school closed when the town's other grammar schools all merged in to new premises at Cocklebury Road.[23]

The Old Grammar School building was a former cloth mill, built in 1788 by Henry Barnet, closing in 1811.

George Goldney Marks established his 'Aerated Water Works' here c1872. This was taken over by Francis Holland c1884, then Herbert Edward Corner from 1905 to 1910 for his 'Mineral Water Works'. Finally, it was occupied by Arthur James Taylor until closure in 1956. It has since been converted into apartments.[24]

---

[22] Wiltshire Times & Trowbridge Advertiser, 11 July 1953.

[23] Wiltshire Times, 27 August 1955.

[24] http://westcountrybottles.co.uk/mike4/P1.html

In the centre of the Market Place is **The Shambles**. This name comes from an old Anglo Saxon word *Scammel*, which was a bench or wooden table where meat was cut and then presented for sale.[25] Originally, these tables were in a long shed with oak timber supports, covered by a stone tiled roof, that was 31 yards long and 13 feet wide. Eight butchers regularly journeyed in from the surrounding villages to sell their meat there.
In 1856, these stalls were pulled down and burned in the Market Place. The rest of the buildings in Shambles were gutted by a severe fire in 1892.[26]

Numerous public houses were here including the 'Red Lion', 'Sun' and 'Three Cups'. The 'Sun' was completely destroyed by fire in 1838, under suspicious circumstances. Nine days before its final demise, a similar fire had occurred but was noticed in time to put out, as it began much earlier in the night than the second fire.[27] The 'Three Cups' behind, was ran by Richard 'Dicky' Fry.[28] Dicky also had a Ginger Beer factory on site, and was landlord from 1830 until 1886 when Francis Holland took over changing the name to 'Shambles Hotel'.[29]

The Buttercross in its original position.

The Buttercross, which was restored in 1995, was originally situated in the Shambles where Barclays Bank is now. It was taken down in 1889 and the sold for £6 to Mr Lowndes of Castle Combe to use as a summer house in the grounds of the Manor. The Buttercross, or Buttery, was a stall with stone pillars, where butter was sold that was built c1570.[30]

---

[25] Chamberlain, Joseph A, (1976), p.6.

[26] Chamberlain, Joseph A, (1976), p.6.

[27] Berkshire Chronicle, 3 February 1838.

[28] White, George A.H., (1924), p.18

[29] http://westcountrybottles.co.uk/mike4/P1.html

[30] Baines, Richard, (2009), p.120.

Next to the Shambles, is the original town hall complete with court room and lock up. This is called the Yelde Hall, which means 'Guild Hall', and is now a Grade I listed building. Dendrochronological dating of the timbers shows that the hall must have been built c1450, so would have existed at the time of the Town Charter in 1554.

During the reign of Henry VIII, it was given by the King to Katherine Parr as a wedding gift. The hall was then sold by the Crown during the reign of Edward VI to Lord Darcy (see Darcy Close), who in turn sold it to Sir W Sherrington. This sale was disputed, as it was believed that the the Crown had no right to sell in the first place.

Pressure was put on Sherrington to restore rights, and in 1569 he yielded, leasing his tolls of fairs and markets that accompanied the land, to the Bailiff and Burgesses for forty years. This was agreed on the condition that they kept the hall in good repair and allow the Lord of the Hundred to keep his 'Law Day' there once a year.[31]

The Market Place in the 1980s. Photograph - Sasha Berry.

Up to 1580, the hall stood alone in the Market Place, until leases were granted to erect stalls, shops and the Shambles themselves. Two large evergreen trees used to stand in front of the Yelde Hall. The Blind House, or Borough Lock-up, is in a room below the upper main hall. In 1709, the bailiff records record that 'spent with six pirates in custody, one shilling for seven quarts of ale'.[32]

The initials JS, which can be seen below the town coat of arms on the front of the building, belong to John Scott who was Bailiff when the hall was repaired in 1776.

It is the sole survivor of the 1892 Shambles Fire.

Until the 1950s, the northern wall of the hall was hidden by an additional building which was at one time an Thomas Long's Umbrella Hospital and Tobacconists.

On the same side is the Monkton Spring fountain although the water no has ever flowed here. Sir John Neeld gave 100 guineas to carry the water under the river bed to its original location which was next to the town bridge.[33]

---

[31] Daniell, J.J., (1894), p. 63.

[32] Goldney, F.H., (1889), p.239.

[33] Daniell, J.J., (1894), p. 34.

The fountain was moved to John Coles Park, probably after bridge alterations, and then moved to its present site in 1980.

After the new town hall was built in the High Street it had various uses including; an armoury from 1891, a home for the fire brigade from 1911 to 1945, and the town Museum from 1963 to 2000. It then became the Tourist Information Centre, and finally an annex to the Museum.

The Market Place, c1905.

The **Market Place**, as the name suggests, was the site of town market. Some of the original bollards used to tie up livestock can still be found here as well as along the High Street. These were manufactured by Rowland Brotherhood in 1860 at his foundry (see Foundry Lane). At one time they could also be found by the shops at the bottom of Station Hill, for protection against runaway lorries.[34]

The Market Place has always been the heart of the town, and today there are still many public events which include it in some way such as the Remembrance Day Parade and the Christmas lights switch on. In years gone by, bonfires were lit here at times of great celebration, such as coronations and to mark the end of conflict.

The main water supply for the town was at the site of the war memorial. A structure stood over the old town pump which bore the arms of Sir Edward Hungerford on a pediment with the inscription - 'Erected by Sir Edward Hungerford, 1679.' As other wells were dug, it no longer became the only source of water in the town, and fell into disrepair.[35]

By 1767 the town pump was restored and iron rails were put around it for protection.[36]

Both the pump and the fence surrounding it, were removed in 1867 and replaced with a fountain funded by £260 of public subscriptions. Part of this fountain is still present as part of the war memorial.

---

[34] Chamberlain, Joseph A, (1976), p.9.

[35] Daniell, J.J., (1894), pp.86-87.

[36] Goldney, F.H., (1889), p.89.

The water supply of the town had long been a serious concern and in 1869, a letter from a 'Chippenhamite' was published in the Western Daily Press describing the 'Chippenham Fever.' The town had been subject to attacks of the fever for many years, with many dying, permanently disabled or left as 'chattering idiots'. A shortage of clean drinking water was found to be the cause, the inhabitants having to pay for such a privilege. Also poor drainage and a dirty river choked with 'slime and decomposing vegetable matter' added to the problem. The writer cites thirty cases within six weeks, just within his own small social circle.[37] Notable residents who had succumbed to Typhoid Fever that year were Dr. William Henry Colborne and Peter Awdry. Another severe outbreak occurred in 1871, attacking all levels of society, but by then Chippenham folk had become indifferent to the situation.[38]

It was later discovered that the cause of 'Chippenham Fever', or Typhoid as it turned out to be, was sewage entering the water supply through fissures in the rock strata. The closure of public wells and the opening of a reservoir put an end to the problem.[39]

The War memorial replaced this fountain not long after this postcard was sent in 1916.

With public wells closed, the fountain in the Market Place became disused, but it was given a new purpose as part of the new town war memorial, which was unveiled on 23 May 1921.

The idea of a memorial was first discussed by the town council in September 1916, soon after the infamous Battle of the Somme. The church was already keeping a list of names of those who had died, and in April 1919 a committee was set up to organise a permanent memorial. The committee put forward the idea of buying Monkton Park house and grounds, to turn them over for public use a memorial park. This was an unpopular idea as it was seen as commemorating those who had died, in a 'pleasure ground'. Ultimately the idea was rejected due to cost and because it was felt a permanent memorial would be more acceptable. A public competition was launched for the design. Rejected ideas included a pathway of lights over the town bridge, 'workmen's houses' with

---

[37] Western Daily Press, 24 November 1869.

[38] Devizes & Wiltshire Gazette, 7 September 1871.

[39] Daniell, J.J., (1894), pp.86-87.

streets named after battles, a memorial in Birds Marsh or an enlargement of the Cottage Hospital. The most popular suggestion was to record the names of the fallen on a memorial in the Market Place incorporating the old fountain. The cost of the design by Mr Parker-Pearson of Grittleton was £785.[40]

The names of those who died in the Second World War were added to the memorial in 1954. The War Memorial Committee managed to ensure their addition, rather than have a separate 'illuminated roll of honour' hidden away in a cabinet in the council office entrance as originally planned.[41]

The church of St Andrew has a long history as there has been a place of worship here for over 1,000 years. Notably, it was the venue for the marriage of King Alfred's sister, Æthelswith, to King Burgred of Mercia in AD 853. This was an important political union at a time of great unrest in the country.

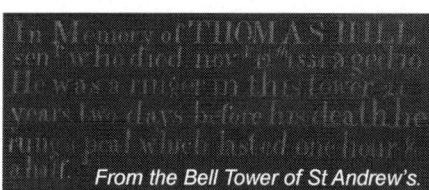
From the Bell Tower of St Andrew's

The original tower was rebuilt at a cost of £320 in 1633, when it collapsed because of constant bell ringing. The building includes St. Katherine's chapel, built in 1760 and paid for by the town's silk manufacturers.[42]

An area was set aside for punishments outside the gates of the churchyard. The pillory and the whipping post are often mentioned in the Churchwarden's accounts, and this was ideally situated to maximise public awareness. Those being punished were in close proximity to the market, church and town hall which was conveniently equipped with the blind house, or town lock up, underneath.[43] Until 1831, the stocks were kept at the northern end of The Butts, facing St Mary Street.[44]

Also in the Market Place, the Jubilee Building was built in 1887 for use as a Literary and Scientific Institute. It was part of the town's programme to commemorate Queen Victoria's jubilee, which also included the planting of a clump of oak trees at the top of the

---

[40] John Belcher from research in Wiltshire Times 1916-1921.

[41] Wiltshire Times, 10 July 1954.

[42] Griffiths, T.J., (1982),

[43] Daniell, J.J., (1894), pp. 80-81.

[44] White, George A.H., (1924), p.14.

Borough land at Englands.[45] The Institute was later used as a Grammar school, and is now the home of Chippenham Borough Lands Charity.[46]

The Market Place was home to a number of public houses many of which have long gone.
The north-facing part of 14 Market Place was the Antelope Inn in 1784. It was no longer a pub by 1829 when it was occupied by James Tanner, a perfumer, and would later become the office of Messrs Tilley and Culverwell.[47]

The King's Head was at 35 Market Place, a Grade II listed 18th-century building next to the entrance to St Andrew's church. At number 37 was the Duke of Cumberland which closed in 1962 and is now Allen and Harris estate agents. Its large cellar juts out from the building and underneath the road in the direction of the war memorial. Before 1750, the Duke of

Girls Training Corps, Market Place, 1944. Photograph - Annie Higgs.

Cumberland was known as the 'Catherine Wheel' and the 'Trooper'. Numbers 38-39 Market Place was formerly the site of the 'Bell Inn', complete with a dome on its roof. The Bell was first mentioned in the *Tropenell Cartulary* of 1320. In 1672 it was owned by Adam Farnewell, alias Goldney; in 1727 it was divided into two properties and by 1750 it was no longer there.
The 'White Lion Hotel' was on the other side of the Market Place at number 3, complete with its own brewery. This is now Sarah Jayne's coffee shop.

As early as 1613, 34 Market Place was an Inn called the 'Lyon'. This was reputedly where John Woodman plotted the Great Fire of London in 1666, and is now part of 'London Buildings'.[48]
There was a 'serious suspicion' that the Great Fire was the result of a plot hatched in Chippenham. When a special committee of the House of Commons set up an enquiry into the cause of the fire,

---

[45] Goldney, F.H., (1889), p.182.

[46] Endacott, F.J., (1978).

[47] White, George A.H., (1924), p.20.

[48] Platts, Arnold, (1947), p.71.

William Duckett MP of Hartham, gave evidence to this fact. On the Thursday before the fire happened, Harry Baker of Chippenham met with John Woodman of Kellaways to discuss a cattle purchase. When Baker asked Woodman if he could hold on until he was ready to buy, Woodman said he couldn't and needed to leave the country but did not want to say why. At the time, it was customary for a bonfire to be lit in the Market Place if there was any cause of a public celebration, and Woodman, when Baker persisted to question him, declared that the 'brave blades' of Chippenham would soon have more of what they desired. Woodman told Baker; 'If you live a week longer you shall see London, as sad a London as ever it was since the world began'. Baker had thought no more of this incident until he heard about the Great Fire. When news reached Duckett, a warrant for Woodman's arrest was issued, but he had already fled the country.[49]

The accepted version is that the fire was caused by accident at the bakery of Thomas Farriner in Pudding Lane.

The White Hart Inn used to incorporate numbers 44 to 48 Market Place, which includes the current Iceland. It is said that both Oliver Cromwell and Robert Peel stayed here before it ceased to function as the principal coaching inn of Chippenham in 1850. Its closure was due to the decline in the coaching trade after the arrival of the railway in 1841.

The frontage of the former White Hart coaching inn survives as part of Iceland supermarket.

The stagecoach was the original high-speed transport network of the early modern era. Carriers held little regard for safety. High speeds were taken and passengers crammed in to maximise profits, and accidents were commonplace. Anstey wrote of one such incident in which he had the misfortune to be involved with. On route to Bath from London, a heavily laden stagecoach broke down at Derry Hill. Many suffered bruises and broken limbs and had to be confined at the White Hart. Ten passengers were inside the coach and a further 16 around the outside including the Guard and Coachman. In addition to this frightful overcrowding, luggage was piled on the roof six feet high.[50]

---

[49] Daniell, J.J., (1894), p.105.

[50] Anstey, The New Bath Guide, 1804.

In 1581, the Inn was known simply as *Ye Harte* and was owned by Philip Smith.

The original structure of the White Hart suggested that it may have once been the mansion of the Lord of the Hundred of Chippenham.[51] Only the facade was retained when it was 'tactfully converted into a supermarket' by the Percy Thomas Partnership in 1970 to 72.[52]

In 1649, a payment was made to Robert Smithers for 'a pottle of sack and a pottle of Clarett which was presented unto General Cromwell when he dyned at the Whyte Hart in his journey towards Bristol for Ireland.'[53] Cromwell also put 400 horses into Westmead, which spoiled the hay crop. It appears from the Churchwarden's accounts, that he then put his horsemen into the church. They record money spent on 'mending a seat which the soldiers pulled down' and 'making clean the church which the soldiers defiled.' The visit must have caused quite an upset in the town, so perhaps when the bells were rung as Cromwell passed through again in 1650, it was not in celebration, but as a warning!

Another notable business in the Market Place, first at number 42 and later at 58, was William Couch's pharmacy. Affectionately known as 'Doc', he made and sold medicines which were exported around the world. He was also a shrewd investor, enabling him to leave a substantial legacy for the benefit others. His daughter was careful with her inheritance and when she too passed away, the 'William Doc Couch Trust', as well as other local charities, benefitted enormously. The trust was set up in 1984 'for the education of needy or handicapped children'.

Many of the older residents of the town will have fond memories of Doc Couch, and he deserves a mention in any history of Chippenham.[54]

The Bear Hotel, Market Place.

The original Bear Inn was at number 11. It was rebuilt in 1750 by Sir Samuel Fludyer. The Bear we see today was once the

---

[51] Daniell, J.J., (1894), p.83.

[52] Pevsner, N., (1975), p.170.

[53] Goldney, F.H., (1889), p.218.

[54] Gazette and Herald, 2 May 2000.

home of Barbara the Polar Bear, late of London Zoo. She was a firm favourite there with visitors until she died in 1923. Her celebrity lived on for a brief time when she was stuffed, sold and put on display outside of the Bear Hotel.[55]

The earliest record of the Angel Hotel was in 1613 when it was known as 'The Bull House'. This was changed to 'The Angel' by 1747.[56] The Angel was bought by Sir Maxwell Joseph of Grand Metropolitan Hotels Ltd in 1958. At one time, stables for up to 120 horses were behind the hotel. In 1959, the new owners built seven 'American motel' style buildings here, designed by Mr RJ Brown. These have since been replaced by the modern extensions present today.

Lord's Lane is the shortest street in Chippenham. It comes off the Market Place between the Rose & Crown and the former Chas Hart Jewellers building, and then joins Timber Street. Lord's Lane was called 'Rose & Crown Lane' on both the 1851 and 1881 censuses. At one time, it was a pedestrian thoroughfare only, but became used as a handy cut through to the Market Place for cars, until the council banned motor vehicles from using the road in 1950.
The Rose and Crown is the oldest surviving pub in the town. Parts of its structure can be dated back to the late 14th Century. It was once known as 'The Barge' due to its proximity to the canal wharf behind, which is now covered over and used as the bus station.

The **Flowers Yard** estate was built by Barrett Homes and is named after George Flower's scrapyard. George was a successful businessman, so much so he became the largest scrap metal dealer in the south west of England. He was also a keen amateur footballer and president of the Westmead Old Boys Association.[57]

George Flower, scrap dealer (far left) at his yard on Gladstone Road. Photo courtesy of Paul and Joy Gough.

Also on the estate, **Fuller Close** is a reminder of a former use of this land. A Fuller was someone

---

[55] Wiltshire Times, 21 July 1934.

[56] Platts, Arnold, (1947), p.69.

[57] Endacott, F.J., (1978),

26

who cleans cloth through a process called 'fulling'. This would have taken place at the mill nearby in Westmead Lane.

The other accompanying street is **Louise Rayner Place.** Louise Rayner, 1832 to 1924, was a British watercolour artist. She visited the town in 1865 and painted a landscape entitled *Chippenham Market Day*. This painting showed the hustle and bustle of the market, and a copy can be seen in Chippenham Museum.

Running parallel with the River Avon, **Westmead Lane** was the home to various factories and was formerly called Factory Lane. Westmead is the name of the land here and is recorded as early as 1245 as *Westmede*.[58]

Messrs. Pocock & Co. opened their cloth factory, Waterford Mills, at Westmead in 1811. Cloth production had already been underway in Chippenham as early as 1707. Pocock's 'West of England' cloth had a worldwide reputation for its excellence of manufacture, confirmed by its award of a gold medal at the Great Exhibition of 1851. It was a widely held belief that 'one could never wear out the cloth'. Notable town resident John Coles used to boast how his overcoat looked 'as good as new' even after fifty years of wear.[59]

St John's Ambulance Cadets receiving First Aid Certificates at Cadet HQ, Westmead, in 1958. Photograph - David Smith.

Waterford Mills was destroyed by fire on 21 May 1915, just as an order had come to the factory for 'a million yards of khaki cloth' for the French Army. This fuelled rumours that the fire was caused by some kind of enemy subterfuge.[60] The fire meant that approximately 200 people were made redundant.

The production of cloth in Chippenham declined and then ceased entirely in 1930, with the remaining machinery taken to Stroud. Part of the buildings at Westmead were incorporated into the tannery which had been established in 1808 by Thomas Bailey.[61] Richard Mortimore was the Tannery Master in 1851, employing 46 men and

---

[58] Gover, J.E.B., (1939), p.83.

[59] Wiltshire Times, 24 January 1931.

[60] Wiltshire Times, 24 January 1931.

[61] Goldney, F.H., (1889), p.123.

4 boys.[62] The tannery continued operations until it was demolished in 1958.[63] A second tannery, which stood on the east side of Westmead Lane, was opened in 1861 by Messrs J & TA Smith. This closed in 1928 and the land become part of George Flower's scrapyard.[64]

The rest of the buildings here were reused when OXO (later Brooke Bond) opened their factory in 1939. This was one of only two factories in the country that made the famous 'OXO Cube'. It closed in 1975 with a loss of 200 jobs.

Afterwards Mattesons (later Hygrade) was one of the town's largest employers until they also closed in April 2007, with a loss of 550 jobs. The factory was demolished in 2013.

Many of the the old 'worker' houses in Factory Lane were condemned before the Second World War and cleared of their occupants. A temporary reversal was required when they were reopened for evacuees.[65] These were eventually demolished, and in 1963 sheltered accommodation was built in their place. This building was going to be called *Westmead House*, but because this was already being used by the occupiers of number 26 Factory Lane, it was changed to *Avonside*.[66]

View of the Paddocks from Westmead.

A new development has now been built across the industrial area by McCarthy and Stone, called Waterford Place after the former cloth mill.

Previously known as Blind Lane, **Gladstone Road** was changed in 1930, despite the objections of Mr EP Awdry, who did not believe in 'wiping out names of bygone days'.[67] The idea for the new name

---

[62] 1851 Census.

[63] Smith, C., (1977), p.20.

[64] Chippenham Through Time.

[65] Comley, CHP. 920, WSHC.

[66] G19/100/20, p.138, WSHC.

[67] Western Daily Press, 9 January 1930.

came from the Gladstone Liberal Club, which was formally opened by public meeting and 'smoking concert' in 1897, and was situated in Blind Lane.[68]
Although John Evelyn Gladstone of nearby Bowden Park was made High Sheriff of Wiltshire in 1897, it was in honour of his uncle, William Ewart Gladstone, that the Liberal Club was given its name. The 'Grand Old Man' of the Liberal party served four terms as Prime Minister during his 60 year career in politics.

In 2006, local architect Jack Konynenburg built four houses next to the Gladstone Arms, and was granted permission by the council to name the access road **Victoria Place** after his late wife.[69] Notably, these were the first houses in the town to be built with 'green sedum' roofs.

Close by there is a public right of way known as 'Bull's Hill' runs between Gladstone Road and Westmead Lane.

Timber street is believed to be the site of King Alfred's 'Palace' although no firm evidence has yet been found. Excavations which took place after the former Gaumont cinema was demolished found nothing to prove the legend. A mound was situated in the gardens of the houses that preceded the cinema, and it was thought to be the site of a watch tower, giving commanding views of the Avon Valley and as far as ten miles around. Foundations of a very old building were also discovered, with a spiral staircase cut in steps out of a solid trunk of a huge oak, which was believed to have originally formed the ascent to a turret of the tower. This was removed site c. 1820, and unfortunately left to decay outside in a nearby timber yard.[70] This have been considered as potential evidence of the Kings *Villa Regia*, and the site has traditionally been known as Palace Square, because of this belief.[71]

The Gaumont was opened in November 1936. This fabulous Art Deco structure became the centre of weekend entertainment in the town until the late 1990's, first as a cinema and later as a nationally renowned music venue and nightclub called *Goldiggers*. The building was the work of William Edward Trent and included three

---

[68] Wiltshire Times, 25 September 1897.

[69] Gazette and Herald, 17 February 2006.

[70] Daniell, J.J., (1894), p. 5.

[71] Platts, Arnold, (1947), p.1.

carved stone panels representing the 'Spirit of Cinema', with 'Light' and 'Sound' either side. These were preserved after the demolition in 2004, and can now be found on the front of Castle Lodge Retirement flats, which was built in its place.

In 1822 during the feast of St Peter, which was a popular event in Langley Fitzurse, rioting took place between its villagers and a group of young men from Chippenham who offended the feast, and caused outrage in the Langleys. On September 7th, between 30 and 40 men 'armed with bludgeons' marched into Chippenham calling out anyone who would dare to fight with them, attacking anyone they met in the street. The Constables and men of the town fought to eject them, and the ensuing battle in Timber Street led to two deaths and thirty one injured, including women and children.[72]

Bakehouse Close is a mixture of houses and flats built by Halsall Construction c1997. It is named after The Old Bakehouse which was on the corner of Timber Street. The standard of the bread made there was very high, and was even recognised nationally when it was presented with a silver medal for its Procea bread in 1952. Procea bread is a type of brown bread which is fortified with protein.

Close by is the start of **Wood Lane**, one of the oldest routes through the town. This was a way that timber was conveyed to the saw pits from Pewsham Forest. The first council houses in the town were built at the far end in 1914.

The old NAAFI building, later Police Station, in Wood Lane.

Westmead Junior school began life as a non-conformist school in 1844, and moved to Wood Lane in 1858, opening on the 10th June. In 1904 It was renamed Westmead Council School. An extension was built in 1907 with funding from the government 'Whisky Tax', which was also used to build Westmead Infants on the opposite side of the road and Ivy Lane School near Foghamshire.

Until the sewage works opened in 1906, the nearby canal had gradually become an open sewer and the smell was often so bad the school windows had to be
kept shut at all times.

---

[72] Daniell, J.J., (1894), p. 107.

The Junior School building was badly damaged by arsonists on 20 January 1972, when the office was destroyed along with many irreplaceable school records.[73]

The combined Westmead Primary School closed in 1989 and the pupils were transferred to the new Kings Lodge Primary School on the Pewsham Estate.

The other end of Wood Lane was to see another new primary school built in 1994 called Charter Primary School. This was needed due to the further expansion of the Pewsham estate.

Westmead Infants School in 'Welcome to the King and Queen'. Photograph - Christine Tombs.

A small non-conformist cemetery is opposite the now boarded up Westmead School building. There was a small chapel at the end of the path, which was used by the Baptists whilst their chapel was undergoing extension work in 1906.[74]

The last burial here was in 1936. The Open Spaces Act 1906 ensured that the cemetery, which was unconsecrated, could only be used as an open space after it's closure.[75] In 1963, work was carried out at a cost of £450, to convert the then disused cemetery into such an open space. The memorial stones were moved to the sides and grass was sown, flowers planted and benches put in.[76] It is now used as a small park, with only a few gravestones still visible.

Wood Lane Non-Conformist Burial Ground, was in use up until 1936. It is now a pleasant open space.

After its break by the Avenue Le Flèche, Wood Lane resumes. **Westmead Terrace** is here and is named after the Borough land it looks across. The access point to **Town Mews** is on the opposite

---

[73] Endacott, F.J., (1978),

[74] Endacott, F.J., (1978),

[75] G19/100/18, pp.275, WSHC.

[76] G19/100/19, p.403, WSHC.

side of the road. 'Mews' is word often given to a building used for keeping horses, so perhaps some were kept here?

Houses in Wood Lane which have been demolished. Photograph - Robin Hardie.

The last thatched cottage in Chippenham was in Wood Lane, until it was demolished in 1939. This was known as Neate's Cottage, as it had been in that family for over two centuries. George Neate, and before him his father William, used to go to Arthur's Well (see Bath Road) to collect spring water, and would sell it for 1/2d a bucket. It was carried around the town in a barrel mounted on a cart, and was a successful venture, until a public water supply was laid on in the 1870's. Neate's old barrel ended up in the Condensery Piggeries at Lowden.[77]

Off Wood Lane, on the 'town end', just after the now derelict former police station, is **The Paddocks.** Half way down the street with a superb view of Westmead playing fields and the Avon Valley, is the Georgian 'Paddocks'. Originally called 'The Paddock', a lodge still exists on Wood Lane. It was divided into six flats in 1961 by EJ Pitt when the modern houses which surround it were built.[78] The Paddock was originally home to the Awdry family (see Awdry Close). The developers EJ Pitt (Builders) Ltd named the new street after the big house.[79]

There were two 'closes' of land under the ownership of the Maud Heath Trust here called 'Horse croft', in the occupation of a Mr Singer in 1757.

The **Avenue La Flèche** was built in 1988 as a relief road for the town centre. It is named after the town of La Flèche which was twinned with Chippenham on 26 February 1983. There was a long dispute over the name with the original choice being 'Avon Way'. The other town twinned with Chippenham is Friedberg, which linked up ten years later on 4 September 1993. The section of the national

---

[77] Wiltshire Times & Trowbridge Advertiser, 1 April 1939.

[78] G19/100/19, p.82, WSHC.

[79] G19/100/19, p.22 & p.52, WSHC.

cycle network which passes through Chippenham is called 'Friedberg Way'.

Cows by the Avon. This is now the Avenue la Flèche. Photograph - Tim Gatherum.

Popham Court is named after Popham's Charity which was setup in 1637. Sir Francis Popham gave land, the profits of which were to be 'distributed to the poor freeman and burgesses at Michalmass each year'. In 1735, the bailiff and borough, were given additional lands at Foxham and 'Dale Mead' in the parish of Christian Malford. The profits were to be distributed between the feast of St Michael the Archangel and the feast of All Saints, during October each year, to six Freemen. These six, would need to be nominated by Popham or his heirs, or if not possible by the bailiff of the corporation. Sir Francis also gifted £40 to go towards the re-edifying of the church tower and steeple.[80] Part of the Popham Charity fund was used for the building of the school at Cocklebury road. The charity is still active today and coupled with Robert Gale's Gift (see Gales Close).

The small social housing estate at **Little Englands** is named after the fields which were part of Borough lands off of Wood Lane. Englands is a modern variant of; *Hinlond* - 1275,[81] *Indeland* - 1514, *Ingelands* - 1604, *Inlands* - 1659.[82]

Burlands Road is built close to the disused canal tunnel which closed in 1912, when the stretch from here to the Wharf in Timber Street became disused.[83] The name 'Burlands', which was chosen in 1916, is a 'contraction of Borough lands'. The purpose of the road having been made with the idea of opening up easier access to the Borough

On the corner of Burlands Road and The Causeway. Photograph - Sarah Teal.

---

[80] Daniell, J.J., (1894), p.161.

[81] Platts, Arnold, (1947), p.7.

[82] Gover, J.E.B., (1939), p.93.

[83] Platts, Arnold, (1947), p.82.

lands.'[84]

The **Causeway** is one of the oldest streets in the town, originally running across low and flat fields and then up to the top of Derry Hill. This land was swampy in ancient times and the pathway was susceptible to floods fed by a small stream called 'The Pewe'. A raised bank pitched with stone was built to make this easier to navigate. The Causeway was mentioned in the Charter of 1554 as *Cawsaye*.[85] The Charter included instruction to raise monies for the improvement and upkeep of the Causeway.

It acquired the name of 'Rotten Row' due to the poor condition of the road surface, when it was maintained as it lay outside the borough boundary. Horse-drawn carriages would turn off by the Three Crowns public house and enter the town via St Mary Street, bypassing the Causeway altogether.

The first Methodist chapel in Chippenham was built on the Causeway in 1812 for the Wesleyans, and used by them until their new church was built at Monkton Hill. In 1909, the vacant chapel was converted by Samuel Spinke as a factory for his printing works and bookselling business, and used as such until 1978. It is now divided into three homes.

The Causeway. The Five Alls Inn is on the right.

The first *Primitive* Methodist Church was on the Causeway, and was a former-schoolroom purchased from the Quakers in 1834. This was much to small for the growing congregation, so a replacement was built in 1896 by John Smith. This was in front of the old church and cost £1,450 to build. Smith's son, John Maitland Smith, was presented with a silver trowel when he lay the memorial stone, and this can be viewed in Chippenham Museum. The last service here was in 1996 when the Primitives joined with the Wesleyan at their church in Monkton Hill, becoming the Methodist Fellowship. The old building is now the home of The Cause Arts Centre.

Another notable business on the Causeway was John Iles & Son, Butchers at number 32. The Iles family began trading here in 1883,

---

[84] G19/100/6, p.152, WSHC.

[85] Daniell, J.J., (1894), p. 58.

taking over a business from another butcher, and stayed on the Causeway until closure in 2017.

Causeway Close is a modern residential accompaniment to the street.

Before improvements were made to the Causeway, **St Mary Street** was on the main route from London so would have been much busier than it is today. Previous spellings include; 'Seynt Mary Strete' in 1514, 'Seynt Maries Strete' in 1561.[86]
The High Street end after the bend was called Cook Street. This bend, which is near The Grove, used to be even narrower and there were many accidents here in the days of horse and carriage. Until it was demolished in 1826, a shed or stable was situated opposite the Old Vicarage which projected into the road, and this added to the drama of passing through.[87]

In 1694, a mineral spring which was 'supposed to be possessed of medicinal virtues' was built over by Judge Holland on the slope in his garden at the Old Vicarage next to the river.[88] This was known as Chippenham Spa. The structure consisted of a four columned Portico. In 1864 it was pulled down and the columns and lintel re-erected in the garden of the Grove.

A passage that leads from the Market Place to St Mary Street through St Andrew's graveyard was known as 'Ambrose Shore' as late as 1897, with a building on the south of this passage known as the 'Trim Tram'.[89] These names have unfortunately fallen out of use but there is a small wooden sign at the start of the passage, high up on the wall that instructs those who enter to - 'Commit no nuisance'.

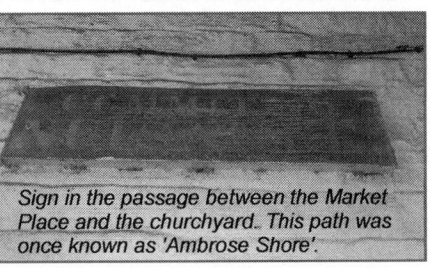
Sign in the passage between the Market Place and the churchyard. This path was once known as 'Ambrose Shore'.

Described as 'one of the prettiest streets in England' by Sir John Betjeman, and 'the best at Chippenham' by Nikolaus Pevsner.

---

[86] Gover, J.E.B., (1939), pp.89-90.

[87] White, George A.H., (1924), p.29.

[88] Daniell, J.J., (1894), p. 34.

[89] Chamberlain, Joseph A, (1976), p.183.

In July 1643, after their defeat at the Battle of Roundway Down, Roundheads who were staying in Chippenham, killed William Iles of Stanley when he crossed their path in St Mary Street.[90]

It is believed that at one time, twelve houses just beyond the borough limit in St Mary Street where it meets with Ladds Lane, belonged to the Manor of Ogbourne St George near Marlborough. This meant that the occupiers were exempt from the laws of the borough and often offenders would use them to avoid the constables.[91]

66 St Mary Street, which was previously in Cook Street, was the house of Richard Scott. His will of 1661 left the property for the use of a schoolmaster 'if a school should be established'. William Woodroffe, yeoman, left in his will of 1664, an annuity of £5 to be paid each year out of profits made from lands in Chippenham called 'The Breach' for a schoolmaster to teach ten boys. These two acts combined led to the establishment of a 'Free School' in the house by Scott's great-grandson in 1733. Between 1834 and 1859, this house was used as the school house and the actual home of the schoolmaster. Ten boys were taught using Woodroffe's gift and a further two boys using the interest accrued on a 1764 gift of £10 from the Mary Bridges estate.

St Andrew's National day school was next to the church between 1837 and 1906, in a building built by John Darley. This was the new building for the National school which had began in 1824, but had needed a larger premises to accommodate up to 500 children. In 1825, the Rev W Short requested a subscription towards the support of the 'lately established National School' from the Borough Council, but due to the state of their finances at the time they turned him down.[92] In 1858, in the large upper room which is level with churchyard, over 100 mixed children were taught by the headmaster, and below in the lower room, at the St Mary Street level, over one hundred infants were taught by a school mistress.

The original vicarage was attached to St Andrew's churchyard until 1826, when it was exchanged for the property on the other side of the street, now the 'Old Vicarage' care home at that time owned by

---

[90] Daniell, J.J., (1894), p. 132.

[91] Daniell, J.J., (1894), p. 112.

[92] Goldney, F.H., (1889), p.142.

Ebenezer Fuller Maitland. This was done so that the original vicarage garden could be used as an extension to the graveyard. For the purposes of the exchange, the vicarage was valued at £675 and Mr Maitland's house at £1,020, so he received £300 for the garden. In 1964, land further down the street was acquired for the current vicarage at 54A St Mary Street.

Baydons Lane runs from the end of St Mary Street to Long Close. Previous recorded variations of Baydons include; Baintons (1736), 'Baidens' (1737), 'Baytons' (1778), 'Bayntuns' (1740), 'Baydons' (1744-1800) and 'Bayntuns' (1800). The lane is named after the Bayntun family (see Bayntons Gardens). Part of Baydons lane was called the 'World's End'. The World's End is described as 'a certain causeway to the corner of Little Black Close' in 1821.[93]

Coming off St Mary Street, just before Baydons Lane begins, is **Common Slip**. The Common Slip used to be a shallow crossing place across the River Avon, also used to wash laundry, and could be used as a ford to cross over into the Monkton Park Estate.
On Powell's map of 1784, a route is marked from Monkton Manor House, and across the river to Common Slip. This is labelled as the Church-way and tells us that this was at one time a route used when attending St Andrews. Indeed, the family at the manor house had its own pew reserved in the church, as was common practice for the upper classes at the time.[94] Also, a pathway existed on the south side of Common Slip before the present wall of the field called Little Black Close was built, manorial documents called this 'The Church-way'.[95]
The crossing at the ford often became treacherous when the river was high. Samuel Fletcher was swept of his horse and drowned in 1795.[96]

Medieval laws obliged all able-bodied men to be proficient in the use of a longbow in case they were called upon for the defence of the realm. **The Butts** was one of two medieval sites, the other was at The Ivy, that were used for archery practice. By decree of the bailiff and burgesses of the town, every householder was bound to help in

---

[93] Chamberlain, Joseph A, (1976), p.9.

[94] Platts, Arnold, (1947), p.67.

[95] White, George A.H., (1924), p.14.

[96] Griffiths, T.J., (1982),

the repair of the both of these.[97] From 1736 until 1860, archery butts are recorded as being kept at Rowden.

Between 1736 and 1739 the Parish Workhouse was in Ladds Lane, until it was given up and its contents sold. By 1753 it had reopened at Mac's Yard (numbers 10-12 The Butts).[98] This three storey building was extended when a former cloth mill here belonging to Henry Elliot, closed in 1825.[99] In 1851, George and Elizabeth Bradbury are recorded as running the workhouse at The Butts, and responsible for 132 inmates.[100] The Workhouse closed in 1859 when a new and larger facility was built at Rowden Hill. It was likely that the conditions of the early workhouse were pretty grim.

Residents of London Road, Causeway and the Butts celebrate the 1937 Coronation of King George VI. Photograph - Debbie Hood

Inmates would be given only the basic essentials and were expected to work hard for their keep. The old workhouse building partially collapsed in 1907 whilst it was being used as a corn store by Messrs. Collen & Brothers of Chippenham mill.

There is a narrow passage between The Butts and Baydons Lane which was once known as 'The Drunj'. Other examples of this unusual name are recorded in Potterne and Bath.[101] This is an example of a name which has either disappeared due to rebuilding or because it may not have been recorded on maps and then forgotten.

The town stocks were at the junction of The Butts and St Mary Street until 1831, when they were moved to London Road, close to the site of the former Cottage Hospital.[102] They were intentionally re-

---

[97] Daniell, J.J., (1894), p. 76.

[98] http://www.workhouses.org.uk/Chippenham/

[99] Baines, Richard, (2009), p.114.

[100] 1851 Census.

[101] Chamberlain, Joseph A, (1976), p.10.

[102] Jefferies, S., (1987), p.83.

positioned as the borough boundary moved, so that outsiders could see that local laws were expected to be adhered to.

During the first half of the 18th century, **Ladd's Lane** was known as *Joseph's Lane.* Its route follows the original town boundary. It is likely that when the lane was renamed, it was after the Ladd family. A Henry Ladd kept sheep at Westmead in 1609.[103] There was also a Luke Ladd listed as a Clothier in Chippenham in 1784.[104]

The Cavaciuti's had their ice cream factory here. This Italian family settled in Chippenham before the Second World War and had various businesses in the town, including the Waverley Cafe and a fish and chip shop in the Market Place, which are still fondly remembered.

A British (non-conformist) school opened in Ladds Lane in 1844, but soon moved to Wood Lane in 1858. This school was the early incarnation of what later became known as Westmead School.

Today, Ladds Lane is a quiet residential street with little evidence of it former uses.

---

[103] Goldney, F.H., (1889), p.37.

[104] Bailey's British Directory, 1784.

3 - Over the Bridge

One of the oldest streets in the town is **Foghamshire**, which was originally part of the main route through from the Bath direction towards Langley Burrell.
Recorded variations of this unusual name include; 'Fokena juxta Chyppeham' (1289), 'Fokenstreet' (1370), 'Foggamshyre' (1514) and 'Foggamshire' (1587).
In the Lacock Cartulary of 1232, a tributary of the river Avon here was mentioned as 'Aqua quaue vocatur Fokena' or 'the stream which is called Fokena'.[105] This tributary is now called Hardenhuish Brook. 'Fokena' derives from *Facnea* which is an old English word for a 'treacherous stream which unexpectedly changes course and size'. This seems a likely explanation to how the name came about as floods used to be a common occurrence here.
An example of this occurred in February 1943, when flash floods struck the town. Small streams became 'raging torrents' with Hardenhuish Brook unable to carry the water away because of the huge volume of water. The fast flowing water and debris became a fascination for the local children. Tragedy almost struck when a four year old girl fell into the stream under the British Restaurant in Audley Road, and was immediately swept away. Fortunately, Allan Norman of Downing Street cycled further downstream to Bath Road, and waited for her.

This Grade II listed building in Foghamshire is one of many surviving small houses in the town with undisputed character.

Miraculously, the girl was pulled out a quarter of a mile from where she fell in. Mr Norman undoubtedly saved her life and received high praise from the mayor at the next town council meeting.[106]

Another curious incident occurred at the point where Foghamshire meets New Road and the bottom of Monkton Hill. One day in 1933, just after a large lorry passed the spot, a three feet wide hole

---

[105] Chamberlain, Joseph A, (1976), p.9.

[106] Wiltshire Times and Trowbridge Advertiser, 13 February 1943.

appeared in the centre of the road. A crust of Tarmac two inches thick was left, but below a 'yawning cavern' approximately ten feet deep and large enough to fit two small cars opened up. The cause was believed to be a defect in the storm overflow sewer and the subsequent continual swirling of flood and storm water in a giant whirlpool underground. Fortunately no one was hurt. [107]

Buildings of note in Foghamshire include; The Constitutional Club, which was built in 1909 and is a two storey Grade II listed building, boasting the Chippenham Borough coat of arms on its facade.

Providence Terrace near to Brunel's Western Arches and in front of Ivy Lane School.

Built on the site of a pub called the Apollo Inn in 1863, is the Temperance Hall. This was an amusement arcade until recently when it became the home of a martial arts school.

The 'Prudential building' is on the opposite corner of Foghamshire and New Road. This Neo-Classical building, with a lead dome on its corner bay, was built c1904 using Hartham Park Stone. The ground floor was a retail business run by Messrs. Foreman, whilst the two upper floors were used by Francis Holland as a cigarette, cigar and snuff factory staffed predominately by young girls. This closed in the 1920s and later became an office for Prudential Insurance. It is now occupied by small retail units including Shoestrings takeaway. Honnibal's Fruit and Veg shop and before that the Anchor Inn were here before it was built.

In 1930, work began on a new hall and offices for the Cooperative society. The foundation stone was laid by Mayor HR Angel in July of that year. This is now the Salvation Army building.

The direction of the main road to Bath has changed significantly since before the advent of toll roads. **Bath Road** is first recorded as 'Batheweye' c1300.[108]

Originally, the 'Bath Way' turned up to Lowden from the Ivy and joined up with what is now Lowden Hill and then Sheldon Road, before going towards Corsham. These days it acts as part of the A4

---

[107] Wiltshire Times, 1 April 1933.

[108] Gover, J.E.B., (1939), p.89.

from London to Bristol. It starts at the Bridge and runs up and over Rowden Hill, past Lowden and towards Corsham.

The first 'modern' version of Bath Road, was built and maintained by the Brickers Barn Turnpike Trustees. In 1792, in order to straighten the Bath to Chippenham section, they applied to the Borough Council for use of part of Littlefield which was Borough land. The council duly agreed at a price of 42 shillings per acre.[109]

There was an old toll house next to the Bath Road railway bridge at the junction with Patterdown, but this was demolished after it was hit by a lorry in 1965. This house was built in the 1850s by local mason James Deacon.[110]

At the town end of Bath Road, stands what is left of the Condensed Milk Factory. This was formerly the site of the Bridge Mill which opened in 1811 with accompanying dye house and shear shop. In 1825 it was used as a silk factory until 1839 when it was used for the storage of hides.

The Anglo-Swiss Condensed Milk Company took over the premises in 1873, and it became their first factory in Britain. In 1905 the company merged with Nestlé. At the time, it was the largest factory of its kind in Europe and employed a large number of local people. In 1913 the 'sweating conditions' at the factory made national news when 200 men and women walked out on strike over hours and pay. For a 60 hour working week, men were paid 18 shillings and women 11 shillings. During the summer hours this increased to 90 hours for 25 shillings, with no overtime rate.[111] When two employees tried to encourage others to join the workers union asking for better conditions, they were dismissed, which in turn ignited the strike.[112]

Francis Hunt of 2 Brook Street, is pictured here (third from left) with his colleagues outside the factory. Photograph - Adrian Denham.

In 1935, the factory became the first stainless steel condensing plant in the country when it was fully modernised. During the war, it

---

[109] Goldney, F.H., (1889), p.104.

[110] Cam Blake, Chippenham Street Names page.

[111] Daily Herald, 13 January 1913.

[112] Daily Herald, 7 January 1913.

was used for the production of Red Cross parcels which were sent to Prisoners of War.[113]

Plans were submitted to build a tunnel under Bath Road for Nestles in the 1950s. This would have helped with the problem of moving cans between the two parts of the factory, which had become increasingly difficult as the road became more used by traffic.

The factory closed in 1962 when production was moved to a purpose-built factory in Cumberland. Now the remaining buildings are used as offices called 'Avonbridge House'.

The Swiss-style 'Bank House' opposite, is a leftover of the factory. It was used as the manager's and wages office. It is so called, not because of its former financial purpose, but because it was built on the bank of Hardenhuish Brook, which was later culverted. Bank House is now used as office space and is an architecturally pleasing

Bank House, opposite Avonbridge House, stands on the bank of the culverted Hardenhuish Brook.

Arthur's Well was once accessible near the now cleared Bridge Centre site, at the end of the wall that used to enclose Nestles Milk factory. This 'Chalybeate Well' supplied generations with an inexhaustible supply of pure mineral water containing iron salts. It was reputed to possess 'ocular qualities' similar to those at the Starwell near Biddestone.[114]

The Bridge Centre was built on the site of the 'Little Ivy', which like its parent Ivy House, was built in the 18th-century Baroque style. One of the Little Ivy's final uses, was as a drill hall for the Territorials during the First World War.

At the start of Bath Road, is the former Salvation Army Citadel. This building is on the corner next to Oxfam. The foundation stones were laid by Frank Fields and Sir John Goldney on 19 September 1903. The Salvation Army were not always popular, and its leader was once 'almost thrown from the town bridge'.[115] The first attempt to establish a Salvation Army corps in the town was in December

---

[113] Platts, Arnold, (1947), p.82

[114] Roberts, 1946, p.197.

[115] Griffiths, T.J., (1982),

1881, when meetings began to be held despite regular disruptions and even occasional violence from the townsfolk.
General Booth and the Salvation Army visited Chippenham in 1884 and did not receive a warm welcome, but when they returned in 1904 the story was completely different. In Chippenham its support grew in greater number than other towns of a similar size.
Previous meeting places before the Citadel hall was established included a premises under the railway viaduct and the Temperance Hall in Foghamshire. In 1971 the 'Sally Army' returned to Foghamshire. The Citadel which had been their home for 67 years, had become too small for their needs and was prone to flooding.

Back Avon Bridge crossing between River Street and Lovers Walk and onto the Ivy Fields, c1905.

Lovers Walk is a footpath that originally ran from Bath Road to River Street via the Back Avon footbridge. The Back Avon Bridge was the site of many drownings, as when the fast moving river flooded, those crossing, or even the bridge itself, could get washed away. It is interesting that such a tragic spot had a romantic association!

Richard I charged Rowden Manor with a pension of £7 10s to be paid to 'Hodreve the Nurse'. She was reputedly Richard's wet-nurse and the pension was in recognition of services rendered. King Edward I later allocated £5 of this to the monastery of Ivy Church near Clarendon for its upkeep. The land which provided this annuity became known as 'The Ivy', and this is how **Ivy Lane** gained its relatively recent name.[116]
Ivy Lane was 'Winnick's Lane' on Powell's map of 1784, and 'Frank's Lane' on the Ordnance Survey map of 1886.

Ivy House is hidden behind large wooden gates and a high wall, opposite the site which the Bridge Centre stood. Pevsner described it as 'by far the most interesting, if not the most perfect house of Chippenham'.[117] The original Ivy House was built c1629 by a member of the Scott family, who were the leading clothiers in the

---

[116] Chamberlain, Joseph A, (1976), p.6.

[117] Pevsner, N., (1975), p.172.

town at that time.[118] The existing structure was built in 1728, a remodelling of the first, for John Norris who was lawyer and MP for Chippenham in 1713.
William Northey imported trees direct from North America to plant in the twenty acre grounds of Ivy House, before he died in 1770.[119] These can be best seen on the approach from Rowden Hill.

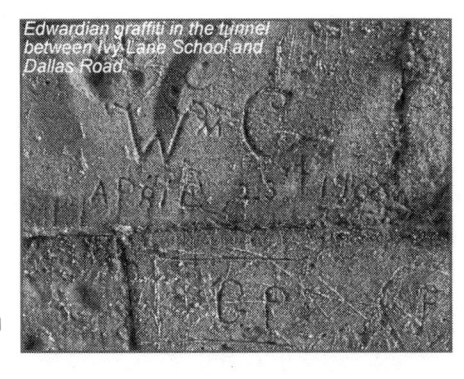

Edwardian graffiti in the tunnel between Ivy Lane School and Dallas Road.

The Ivy was restored in 1981 and is now a Grade I listed building, having been upgraded by the Department of the Environment from a Grade II in 1970.[120]

Ivy Lane School was opened by the council on 7 January 1907 as a replacement for St Andrew's National School in St Mary Street.[121] The school adopted official colours in 1950 - Green and Silver, with an Ivy Leaf as its badge.[122]

Barley Close Lane was between Ivy Lane and where the railway was built, and the remaining properties here are now called **Ivy Cottages**. This was named after two fields, Upper Barley Close and Lower Barley Close. The original road to Bath ran through Barley Close, onto Lowden Hill and then Sheldon Road.

Alec Stone of Woodlands Road. Photograph - Carole Brittain

Ivy Road is also close by. A laundry was built here in 1901 by the Chippenham Sanitary Laundry Company Ltd. At the time, it was estimated that a million gallons of water would be needed for its

---

[118] Baines, Richard, (2009), pp.120-1.

[119] Daniell, J.J., (1894), p. 35.

[120] G19/100/23, p.423, WSHC.

[121] Endacott, F.J., (1978).

[122] Wiltshire Times, 11 March 1950.

operation each year.[123] This was taken from the town supply, and was softened before use. Within a year of trading, they already had fifty customers on their books, under the management of Manageress Miss Coldbeck.

W. Love & Sons, New Road. Photograph - Ann Brinkworth.

New Road was known as the 'Marshfield Turnpike Road' when it was first laid down in 1792 by the Chippenham Turnpike Trustees. It could then be used as an alternative route to Old Road and Monkton Hill, which was a through road before the railway line was built in c1839. New Road was built through an arable field known as the 'Quarry Ground', belonging to Ralph Hale Gaby, who was a Solicitor in the town. The land was purchased by the Trustees for £353 in 1791. Before the road was built there was an old narrow track which ran between the Little George Inn, along what is now the north-west side of the course of the road, to Sambourne farmhouse, near what is now Ivy Lane school. This lane was called 'Brewers Lane', with the land to the north belonging to the Ashe family, called 'Little George Mead'.[124] Travelling circuses used to set up here when they visited Chippenham.

It is believed that Sambourne farmhouse wasn't demolished to make way for the railway embankment, rather it was buried intact underneath it!

In 1925 it was decided to install posts along the pavement on New Road opposite the bottom of the steep Station Hill. This was to protect pedestrians and property from any potential runaway horses or vehicles coming down. The possibility of chains across these posts, was also discussed, but there was a concern that it would be 'an invitation to 'Chippenham Loafers' to sit there and spend the money they got from the dole, in a silly way'.[125]

In 1938, plans had been made for a new cinema in New Road. This would have meant there would have been three cinemas in

---

[123] Wiltshire Times & Trowbridge Advertiser, 20 July 1901.

[124] Wiltshire Times, 1 September 1923.

[125] Wiltshire Times & Trowbridge Advertiser, 9 May 1925.

operation in the town. The plans were eventually rejected by the council due to concerns over the location creating a traffic problem.

The original Police station was in New Road, opposite the junction with Union Road. James Wright was the Police Superintendent in 1859.[126] Later it moved to Park Lane before taking over the old NAAFI building in Wood Lane.

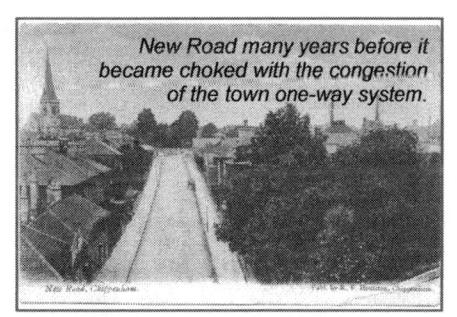

New Road many years before it became choked with the congestion of the town one-way system.

In 1966, the Chamber of Commerce proposed that the section of New Road from the Western Arches to The Bridge, should be renamed High Street. This was rejected, due to the difficulties of renumbering properties and the lack of proven benefits to be gained from the scheme.[127]

Mr W Light's carpentry shop and timber yard in New Road was destroyed by fire in the 1890s. Light never recovered from the shock and died on 31 December 1899.[128]

Orwell House is now part of The Brunel pub which opened in 2000. This was once home to Rowland Brotherhood and his large family. They called their home 'Viaduct House' due to its proximity to Brunel's Western Arches. Brotherhood used one archway as a stable and another as a gymnasium for his ten sons.[129]
Between 1901 and 1912, Orwell House was used as a school ran by Mr Bardwell. Later, the front of the property was extended for use by Hinder's cycle shop and from 1935 until 1993 it was Barrett furnishers.

An example of Phipps Iron work on an entrance gate to London Road cemetery.

---

[126] Post Office Directory, 1859.

[127] G19/100/21, p.376, WSHC.

[128] Wiltshire Times, 24 January 1931.

[129] Jefferies, S., (1987), p.55.

Before the railway was built, **Old Road** was the original route into Chippenham town centre from the direction of Langley Burrell, joining up to Monkton Hill. Also, before the town bridge was strengthened to take the weight of modern wagons, this was the main route from Bath towards London. River crossings also took place at Cocklebury by means of a ford, and joined the present day London Road after Hardens Copse by the turning for Stanley (see Hardens Mead).[130]

Hathaway's Churn Factory was off Old Road from 1869. The wrought iron entrance gates were still there in 1982, and displayed the manufacturers name 'HG Phipps, Chippenham, 1899'.[131] An example of Phipps iron work still exists at London Road cemetery.

Old Road was also the access point for Harding & Son's coal yard, which opened in 1840 with the coming of the Great Western Railway. Frederick Mortimore became a partner in the business in 1889. Not long after, Hugh Harding passed away, leaving Mortimore as sole owner.

Peter Mortimore was the last in the family to run the business, doing so from 1943 until its closure in 1980. The remaining office and weigh-bridge are listed buildings and a charitable organisation called The Weighbridge Trust are hoping to preserve these for future generations.

Union Road. The Chippenham Auxiliary Fire Service formed 1938. Arthur Cook is second on the left. Photograph - Jean Cook.

Old Road and New Road are joined by **Union Road**. It is this union of these two roads which inspired its name. Richard Slade's brewery was here from 1890 to 1926.

Monkton Hill was formerly known as Black Horse Lane (or Hill). The Black Horse Inn used to stand where the Wesleyan Methodist chapel is today. The site was purchased by the Methodists in 1900, and construction began in 1902, continuing until 1908. 1040 cubic feet of rock had to be excavated before the

---

[130] Chamberlain, Joseph A, (1976), p.8.

[131] Griffiths, T.J., (1982),

foundations could be laid. The total cost of construction was £5161 13s and 6d, and it officially opened in April 1909.[132]
Avon Reach offices are on the opposite side of the road of the Methodist church, standing on land reclaimed from the river.

Monkton Hill was also the approach to the main drive for Monkton House. There are three 18th-century limestone gate piers at the entrance of the council offices that mark the start of where this long drive to Monkton House used to begin. A lodge stood on the left hand side, but this has made way for an electric substation.
The original council offices were built between 1965 and 1967 by Burroughs & Hannam, with their replacement coming in 2001 (see Monkton Park).

At the foot of **St Mary's Place** is Ruskin Cottage, with a terrace of seven properties attached, all built by Rowland Brotherhood for his employees. Dating from the 1850s, they are in a similar style to his other terrace at 52-67 Marshfield Road. These buildings are numbered 1 to 7 St Mary's Place.

The narrow street is, as the name would suggest, the site of a former Catholic chapel. This was built in 1855 at a cost of 24 Guineas, during a time when there were few Catholics living in Chippenham and little support for their arrival. The chapel was built largely due to the efforts of two converts; Richard Hungerford Pollen and Elizabeth Sophia Fellowes. Unlike other areas, the town did not receive a large influx of Irish immigrants fleeing persecution and famine, so most of the early Catholic families were converts. A small school was set up here in 1855 with Miss Elizabeth Twomey teaching 10 girls and 8 boys until 1866.

Circus Elephants pass St Mary's R.C. Church on Station Hill, 1951. Photograph - Adrian Hillier.

The land opposite, which was to become the site of the present church and presbytery, was bought by Bishop Clifford in 1869 for £450. This land remained empty until 1901 when Father Bailey acquired £544 in funds for a permanent residence built by Hulberts of Chippenham. Before the Presbytery was built, priests had to find rented accommodation. The first priest, Father Larive, lived in New Road in a house on the site of the former Shamrock Linen Shop.

---

[132] 100 not out!, 2009

The King and Queen passing through Chippenham on 20 July 1907.

This house was used by the priests up until 1893, when Father Bailey moved to 2 Weston Villas, which was one of the former Brunel built homes demolished to make way for the DWP building in Marshfield Road.

The chapel was the first place of worship for local Catholics since the Reformation, and was built despite numerous campaigns over the years to prevent it. Even royalty had to make do during times of forced austerity for Catholics. The King of Portugal (1904) and the King of Spain (1905) are both believed to have worshipped in the tiny chapel whilst on visits to Bowood.

The new Catholic Church was built in 1935, thirty four years after the Presbytery was completed next door. It cost £2,192 and 20 shillings, and officially opened in 1936. The small congregation was soon boosted by an influx of Irish workers and Italian POWs, many of whom decided to stay after the Second World War.

CHIPPENHAM — On display in Chippenham Museum.

The Great Western Railway, designed and built by Brunel, reached Chippenham when the Hay Lane terminus to Chippenham section was opened on 31 May 1841. The first train to arrive here however, was the day before, when a trial trip took place that caused 'no small amount of excitement' amongst the locals.

There had been difficulties involved in the construction of the railway right up until its opening, including landslips from the embankment further down the line.

The original Railway Station was built in 1848, but the existing buildings are from 1858. This was a rebuild by Rowland Brotherhood, using excavated stone from Brunel's famous Box Tunnel.

A few years later, on Monday 25 April 1864 on route to Devon, General Garibaldi the great Italian hero arrived on the 11.40 Express train. A huge crowd filled the platform to see the famous military leader, who had helped to unify Italy. The crowd cheered, people tried to shake the General's hand, and a Royal salute by a cannon made at the Brotherhood foundry, was fired by Rowland's sons. This shattered the glass in the station roof, much to the amusement of Garibaldi and others present. Garibaldi, wearing his well known red jacket, bowed to the people whilst the train stayed for several minutes, and seemed pleased with his welcome.[133]

The Prince of Wales visited Chippenham in March 1902 with the station approach decorated for the occasion. Permission was sought from GWR to plant trees along the sides of the road in commemoration of the visit, and to change its name from 'Station Road' to 'Princess's Avenue'. An avenue of Horse Chestnuts were indeed planted and the road name changed, but in fact it was 'Prince of Wales Hill' which was chosen.[134] Later this was changed to **Station Hill** and this remains so today.
There was a row of six houses at the top of the hill, demolished in the 1970s, which explains the kink in the road. This is evidence of the pre-railway route, which originally started in Old Road and then joined at the top of Station Hill, and then on to Monkton Hill. The 1886 Ordnance Survey map marks these six houses as 'Railway Cottages'. In 1966 these houses were offered to the council by British Rail, but they declined.[135]

The 'Albany Ward Picture Palace' began showing films on Station Hill c1913. The cinema had a 'reputation amongst its clientele for the number of rats it housed', which were probably attracted by the adjoining railway storehouse. In 1921 the building was severely damaged by gales, with a wall and the roof needing to be rebuilt. Eventually the Palace was abandoned in 1936.[136] In 1938 proposals were put forward to completely renovate and then re-open the cinema, but this idea was dropped. Now there were two other cinemas in town (the Astoria opened in 1939) and it was thought that the Palace would not be able to survive.

The Picture Palace after it was hit by a Gale in 1921. Postcard - Jackie Harding.

Next door, was used as a roller skating rink c1910. During the First World War soldiers were billeted here before leaving the town by train. The conditions led to a severe outbreak of measles in 1916. After the war, when the roller skating craze had ended, the building

---

[133] Wiltshire Independent, 28 April 1864.

[134] Western Daily Press, 6 March 1902.

[135] G19/100/21, p.285, WSHC.

[136] Griffiths, T.J., (1982),

was used for Burridge's Garage, later Taylor's Motorcycles, and now is the home of Dorothy House Hospice Furniture Shop. William Burridge bought Chippenham Motor Works in 1913. Originally from Goodleigh in Devon, Burridge spent most of his time between his Station Hill premises, the golf course and his home Ivy Park House on Rowden Hill.

4 - London Road

The residential section of road from Chippenham towards Calne is called **London Road**. This is one of original main routes through the town and now forms part of the A4 from Bristol to London. A Hermit lived in a small dwelling known as the Hermitage opposite the Packhorse pub.[137] He was a religious man who would bless travellers and use charitable donations he received to maintain the road.[138] The earliest record of the Hermitage is in 1604.

Chippenham to Calne annual walking race began in 1951.

London Road has many groups of houses with their own separate name, although some have now fallen out of use. Numbers 2-12 are a terrace of three storied weavers cottages, once known as 'Lansdown Place'.
A ten house three storied weaver style terrace at 87 to 105 London Road called 'Victoria Buildings', and 'Moseley Terrace' an eight house terrace, are both recorded on the 1886 Ordnance Survey map, but only the latter still displays its name.
107 to 117 London Road was originally 'Wembley Terrace', consisting of six semi-detached homes built at the end of 1923 by Downing & Rudman. Each came with its own scullery and coal shed, and was probably named after Wembley Stadium which was built in the same year.
'Nelson's Place' was tucked in behind 'Albert Cottages', the entrance to which can be identified by the named entrance pillars on London Road.
The twelve three-bed former council homes built where the pavement raises opposite the car show room, were built on a former nursery in 1933.[139]

---

[137] Daniell, J.J., (1894), p. 97.

[138] Baines, Richard, (2009), p.147.

[139] G19/760/288, WSHC.

A Kingdom Hall of the Jehovah's Witnesses is on the site of a Friends (Quaker) burial ground.
This was surrounded by allotment gardens until they were developed for housing.
London Road has been a prime location for smaller religious groups, when they have been unable to find a suitable base in the centre of town. In 1669, a venue for a meeting house was acquired off London Road by the Quakers Adam Goldney and William Storr. By 1700, the Quakers had also established a burial ground for their private use, opposite the Pack Horse Public House. In 1812, 51 to 57 London Road were converted into a chapel by the Presbyterians, after their previous building located in the Market Place, was pulled down in 1811.[140]
There are lots of smaller streets that branch off London Road. At one time **Queens Square** was a courtyard of houses. These were later cleared and the land used as allotments.

Rural Gardens is on the site of Rural Place, which would have originally sat outside the town boundary. **Glendale Drive** is next. Glendale is an anglicised Gaelic word which originates from the Isle of Syke meaning 'valley of fertile, low-lying arable land'.

The Royal Oak is one of many pubs to have closed in Chippenham.

Royal Oak Close is situated on land set back from London Road, just before the car showroom in the direction of Calne. This is a modern development built in 2004, partly using land that was the garden of the Royal Oak public house. The original building still fronts onto London Road and has been tastefully converted into a private residence. The pub is one of many that have closed down in Chippenham. Others like the Little George and the Five Alls have become restaurants.

Another modern development along this road, is **Larkham Rise.** George Larkham was Parade Marshall for the Chippenham Branch of the British Legion. During the Second World War, George was landlord of the Little George Hotel at the top of New Road. His only

---

[140] Baines, Richard, (2009), p.135.

daughter, Lavinia Larkham, was a member of the National Fire Service in Swindon.

Larkham Rise is a mixture of houses and flats built c1996 by Crest Homes, on the site of the former Cottage Hospital. In 1897, various potential sites were considered for the hospital. Donations for the building fund came from subscribers, including Mr AW Neeld, Miss Ashe and Mr EH Clutterbuck, the latter of which offered a field next to St Paul's Rectory on Malmesbury Road. It was agreed that although well located near a large area of employment, this was not a suitable site. A quiet part of the town was preferred, so instead Clutterbuck donated £100 towards the building fund. Another popular choice was a field at Barley Close, now the home of Ivy Lane school, but the owner Sir Gabriel Goldney could

The Cottage Hospital on London Road.

not free up the land at that time. Carrick Moore, an owner of much of the land locally, was asked to offer a suitable site, and he put forward a piece of land on London Road that was being used as a stone yard by builder John Smith.[141] This was chosen, and Smith was successful in winning the contract to build the hospital over a rival bid from Downing and Rudman.[142] Interior furnishings were chosen by Miss Emily Stevens, who became the first Matron, having previously worked for ten years at Guy's Hospital in London.[143]
The Foundation Stone was laid on 8 November 1897 by Lady Dickson Poynder, Whose husband Sir John Dickson Poynder, was the first to put forward the idea of a cottage hospital for Chippenham, as a permanent commemoration of the Queen Victoria's Diamond Jubilee. The hospital opened in January 1899.[144] The first Chippenham Carnival was held in 1923, in order to raise funds to keep the hospital running. It remained the main fundraiser for the hospital over the years, as the hospital gradually grew and offered more services. In 1932, a women only ward was built by Walter Rudman, and a few years later in 1936, a nurses home was also added.

---

[141] Wiltshire Times, 29 May 1897.

[142] Wiltshire Times, 25 September 1897.

[143] Wiltshire Times, 13 November 1897.

[144] Bath Chronicle, 19 January 1899.

A notable former patient of the cottage hospital was Sir Arthur Henry Rostron, who was the captain of the Carpathia, when it was first ship to reach the stricken Titanic in 1912. Under his command 710 survivors were rescued, including Mary Elizabeth Davison of Chippenham.[145]
Rostron had an illustrious career as Commodore of the Cunard fleet, and was in command of the RMS Mauretania from 1915 to 1926. His achievements were internationally recognised, holding the Freedom of the City of New York, a US Congressional Medal of Honour and Chevalier de la Legion d'honneur.[146]
Rostron was taken ill with gastric influenza whilst visiting friends in Calne, and died at the hospital on 4 November 1940 aged 71. His family believed that his illness may have been brought on by sleeping in the air raid shelter in his garden.[147]

The modern housing at **Phoenix Close** was built on land that was formerly used by Humphrey Simons Engineering, whose buildings there were called the 'Phoenix Works'. Humphries & Son started in the 19th century, with a waggon works just off the Causeway and close to the Three Crowns Public House. In 1946, William Humphries and Hector Simons merged to form Humphrey Simons Engineering. The company went into voluntary liquidation in 1999.

Baynton Gardens is another modern development off London Road, and is tucked behind Bayntun House on what was the gardens for the big house.
The name of Baynton has been corrupted into many different forms including *Baynton*, *Bayntun*, *Baytons* and *Baydons* (see Baydons Lane). The Bayntun family seat was at Spye Park near Bromham, but they owned land in Chippenham, including at one time, The Ivy. During the Civil War, the Bayntun family were Lords of Rowden, and Sir Edward sided with Parliament. His son, Henry Bayntun, was MP for Chippenham from 1685 to 1690.
Notable occupants of Bayntun House itself include; William John Lysley who was born there in 1825 and Edmund Maitland Awdry (see Awdry Close).

Coming off London Road just before the Pack Horse pub, **Black Cross** leads down a steep incline to join with **Long Close**. Both are

---

[145] Wiltshire Times, 9 November 1940.

[146] The Times, 6 November 1940.

[147] Clements, Eric L., (2016), p. 270.

named after field names that were nearby before the Avon Valley Estate was began in 1953. Long Close and Black Cross follow the original route of Baydons Lane, which linked London Road with St Mary Street.
In 1812, Black Cross field was called *Blackus.* Now it is called 'Baydons Meadow' and managed by Chippenham Borough Lands Charity and set aside as a mini haven for wildlife.[148]

Turning right at the bottom of this hill leads to the Chippenham Sea and Air Cadets. This area has been used for recreation by the people of the town since at least the 1870s. It became a designated bathing place, and was used by Chippenham Amateur Swimming Club from their foundation in 1877. Concerns over public health meant that swimming in the river was discouraged after the Second World War, and the club moved to Corsham pool until Chippenham built their own in 1960. One of the many dangers highlighted at the time was the possibility of contracting jaundice because of rats.[149]

Chippenham Sailing Club at Long Close. Photograph - Nicola Pithouse.

The Springs is a modern development built by Westlea housing on land previously used for eight garages, opposite the Sea Cadets on Long Close.

Other streets also built as part of the Avon Valley Estate, are also named after old field names. **Dyers Close**, **Habrels Close** and **Oate Hill** which all branch off Long Close are examples which can be seen on John Powell's map of 1784. Habrels Close was part of the first phase of 55 'traditional homes' built in 1953 by TF Brain & Co., along with Black Cross and the first half of Long Close.[150]

The Close, which is off Wood Lane, is also an old field name.

Buckland Grove is opposite the turning for Cricketts Lane, and is one of the newest streets in the town. Previously this land was the site of the Platinum Renault Showroom and Garage, with the

---

[148] Chamberlain, Joseph A, (1976), p.8.

[149] Wiltshire Times, 11 March 1950.

[150] G19/723/8, WSHC.

Buckland's Garage.
Photograph - Alison Buckland.

freehold remaining under the ownership of the Buckland family for three generations. Edward Algernon Buckland started the original garage in 1925 and the family ran the business until 1999. The Buckland family owned the site until 2009, after which it continued for a few more years as a van rental shop. It finally closed and was sold for housing in 2012.

Cricketts Lane was 'Cricket's Lane' in 1674 and was likely to have been named after a man or family whose surname was Crickett.[151] There was once a small pottery here.[152] On the Powell's map of 1784 it is marked as 'Rooks Nest Lane'.

Derby Close comes off Cricketts Lane backing onto London Road and Wood Lane. This street was built for the council in 1964, and is made up of 'aged persons bungalows'. It was originally meant to be called 'Stanley Close', but the name was changed due to concerns from the Head Postmaster that mail could get mixed up with those for the village of Stanley itself.[153]

Harden's Copse was between London Road and the river Avon. It was cleared to build **Hardens Mead** in 1958, which was known as the 'Hardens Copse Estate' at the time.[154]

Hardens Close is on the opposite side of London Road next to the cemetery. It was originally intended to be much larger than the fifty houses which were built here in 1939. The previous plan drawn up in 1937 by developers Blackford & Son of Calne, was for a straight road with four smaller roads branching off.[155] The choice of names suggested by them was 'Blackford Avenue' or 'Dennis Way', Dennis

---

[151] Platts, Arnold, (1947), p.72.

[152] Endacott, F.J., (1978),

[153] G19/100/20, p.367, WSHC.

[154] G19/100/17, p.38, WSHC.

[155] G19/760/415, WSHC.

being the 'Son' in Blackford & Son. The General Purposes Committee did not favour these and approved 'Hardens Close' instead, also sidelining 'The Hardens' suggested by Councillor Ryan.[156]

During the Second World War Two bombs were dropped behind Hardens Copse by the Luftwaffe, presumably to lighten their load for the journey back across the channel. These bombs remained unexploded and undiscovered, until local resident Tony Crew showed concern when plans were announced for a new secondary school off Stanley Lane. Only six years old at the time, he remembered seeing the bombs fall there in 1942.
Between 13th and 15th February 1998, Operation Crusade was launched to locate the bombs, assess the danger and act accordingly. The decision was made to destroy both, one of which was a 750kg 'Fatboy' bomb, on site using a controlled explosion. 500 homes were evacuated as a precaution, and the bombs were successfully and safely destroyed under the national media spotlight.
The new secondary school eventually opened in September 2001, and was called Abbeyfield due to its proximity to the former Cistercian Abbey at nearby Stanley.

The Turnpike is a small group of houses on the opposite side of London Road than an existing turnpike building, which stands on the corner of Stanley Lane. There are other remnants of the toll road system around the town, including milestones. Turnpikes gave only modest living conditions for the toll collector, often using existing buildings. The purpose-built toll houses were small to keep the cost down and had only one door for security. Despite the large sums of money handled, the occupation of a toll collector was a lowly one. Collectors were usually pensioners or women from poorer families. The turnpike house here was built in 1835 when the turnpikes around the town were reorganised.[157] It was the work of local mason John Woodman, costing £141. Previously the east gate was close to the Three Crowns at the end of the Causeway. There were seven roads controlled by turnpike trusts which entered the town.
In 1727, the earliest toll belonging to the 'Chippenham Trust' began, charging use of the road between Studley Bridge and Tog Hill. This was abandoned in 1743, when the trust decided to manage the road to Pickwick in Corsham instead.

---

[156] G19/100/10, p.373, WSHC.

[157] Baines, Richard, (2009), p.149

Other turnpike trusts controlled roads into Chippenham; the 'Malmesbury Trust' from the direction of Stanton St Quentin in 1756 and the 'Holt Trust' from Lacock in 1762.

Drury's map of Wiltshire from 1773, shows toll gates at the junction of St Mary Street and the Causeway, and at Chippenham Clift on what is now St Paul's Church cemetery. In 1834 toll houses were added on the Stanley turning on London Road, at Hungerdown Lane near Ferfoot House and at Lowden on the corner of Patterdown.

The Chippenham Trust removed their turnpikes in 1870, and by 1877 all other trusts had followed suit.

5 - Monkton Park

The land at Monkton Park was given by Empress Maud, mother of Henry II, to the priory of Monkton Farleigh. The name Monkton means 'Monk's Town', with other spellings recorded being 'Monketon' during the reign of Henry VIII and 'Mounckton' in 1605.[158]

After the dissolution of the monasteries in 1536, Monkton was passed to the Seymour family who kept possession until 1686. The original Manor House was made of timber, which was converted into a stone mansion by tenant William Bayliffe, before it was sold in 1686 to the Esmeade family. In 1787, Esmead Edridge remodelled the house into what we see today.

At one time there was a moat around the house but this has long since been filled in.

The Esmeades held the manor until 1919. when it was sold to the Coventry family.

When Lady Coventry died in 1957, the council purchased the house, later turning it into eight apartments. The wider estate was developed for housing and became known as 'the largest cul-de-sac in England' because of only having one road in and out.

Chippenham open air swimming pool. Photograph - Maf Coathupe.

Part of the estate was kept as parkland. The footpath which runs through the top of the park, follows the original route of the main approach drive from Monkton Hill to the big house. This route remained clear until the North Wiltshire District Council offices were built over the wooded entrance in 1967, with the modern building we see today replacing it in 2001.

The park used to be home to a number of 'magnificent' Elm trees which succumbed to the notorious Dutch Elm disease in the 1970s.[159]

---

[158] Gover, J.E.B., (1939), p.93.

[159] Griffiths, T.J., (1982),

In May 1960, an eight-lane outdoor swimming pool was opened at Monkton Park which held 360,000 gallons of water. Now long gone, the pool is missed by many, and the nature of its demise has been a contentious subject since its closure in September 1988. The Olympiad leisure centre was built alongside the old pool, and the original plan was to keep both, with a water slide linking the two, but ultimately the council decided the maintenance costs were too high.

The Olympiad under construction. Photograph - Tim Gatherum.

During the 1960s and 1970s, most school children in Chippenham learnt to swim in the outdoor pool. A highlight of its thirty years in service came in 1982, when it hosted the popular BBC TV programme *It's a Knockout.*

Cocklebury Road is currently the only access road to the entire Monkton Park estate. Cocklebury was originally a small area separate from Chippenham. The name comes from the small fossil shells or 'petrified cockles' that are found here in the stones of limestone brash.[160] Early variations of the name appear as 'Kokelesberga' in 1181 and 'Cokelbergia', in 1189.[161] [162] Cocklebury Farm, with its 220 acres, provided much of the land for the modern housing at Monkton Park. In 1952, when plans were being set out for the new estate, the farm was occupied by dairy farmer Mr Self and his herd of 80 cows.[163]

The new Wiltshire and Swindon Heritage Centre was opened on part of the old cattle market site in 2007, replacing the Wiltshire Record Office at Bythesea Road in Trowbridge. In 2008 Linden Homes built 265 properties on the rest of this land. The streets here are called **Great Mead** and **Cowleaze**, both of which are the original field names. Across Cocklebury Road is the Charles Church development of **Market Mead** which is much smaller than the cattle market site, but whose name records the former use of the area.

---

[160] Aubrey, 1670.

[161] Gover, J.E.B., (1939), p.105.

[162] Platts, Arnold, (1947), p.89.

[163] F14/424/20, WSHC.

Market Mead is built where the old Hartwell Ford dealership was, formerly Hewitt's and later Earle's of Chippenham.

Cattle markets had to be taken off the streets from 1911 due to concerns about public health, followed by the Livestock Industry Act of 1937 which aimed to improve animal welfare conditions. In 1938 the search began for a new site. Englands was suggested, but because the cattle would have needed to be driven through the town to the railway station, the site at Cocklebury was eventually decided upon. The cattle market was moved to Cocklebury Road between 1951 to 1954. This modern facility became one of the largest one-day markets in the country, before it closed in 2005, moving to Cribbs Causeway near Bristol

This poplar tree on the bend of Cocklebury Road serves as a natural speed restriction.

In 1915, Wiltshire Farmers Ltd built a milk depot and cheese factory on Cocklebury Road opposite the train station car park.[164] This piece of land is now part of the Sadlers Mead car park located behind the Olympiad Leisure Centre. There are currently plans to build a multi-storey car park here

The additional housing towards the river, which was added to the estate c1988, have streets named after golf courses. These are only a short distance away from the Monkton Park nine hole golf course with pitch and putt, which undoubtably inspired the theme chosen. The golf course was designed in 1965. The six streets are **Gleneagles Close**, **Lytham Close**, **St Mellion Close**, **Turnberry Close, Sunningdale Close** and **Wentworth Close**. Turnberry is in Scotland and owned by US President Donald Trump.

Second World War defences can still be found in five places along the Chippenham stretch of the river, including a 'Type 29' pill box on the golf course. These were part of the 100 mile long 'Stop Line Green', otherwise known as the 'Bristol Outer Defence'. This would have acted as one of many defensive fallback positions to be used

---

[164] G19/760/76, WSHC.

in the event of a German invasion. These particular pillboxes were built in 1940, with 47 inch thick hexagonal walls designed to withstand tank fire. There are two more at Rowden Farm, another just past the Black Bridge and one in the back garden of 28 Sadlers Mead.

Sadlers Mead, along with **Brake Mead, Avon Mead, Downham Mead, Matford Hill,** and **Odcroft Close,** are all old field names which can be found on John Powell's map of 1784. The names of Sadlers Mead, Esmead, Downham Mead and Avonmead, were all recommended by the council when they were built in 1958.[165]

The Tinings is another term for a boundary. This name can be found in many towns close to the boundary of a parish. **Boundary Road** has the same origin.

A Tinman called John Downham had a shop in The Shambles in 1833, so its possible that Downham Mead was either owned by or farmed by his family.[166]

Odcroft Close comes from 'Ode's Croft', the spelling having changed over time. This was recorded as 'One half acre lyeth in Cockleborough-field, called Odecroft' in 1835.[167]

Geographical names are also used here; **Eastern Avenue** as the road is on the east side of town and **Riverside Drive** which runs close to the river Avon.

Eastern Avenue. Photograph - Carole Brittain.

Black Bridge Road is named after the former railway bridge close by. This crossed the River Avon carrying the Chippenham to Calne branch line, affectionately known as the 'Calne Bunk'. The bridge was called this because it was built using stained black timber, until it was replaced by steel in 1920.

The line opened on 29 October 1863 with a delivery to Calne which included 100 pigs. Its first journey with passengers came shortly

---

[165] G19/100/17, p.268, WSHC.

[166] Devizes & Wiltshire Gazette, 5 September 1833.

[167] Parliamentary Papers, 1835.

after on 3 November 1863. The pigs were being taken to Harris's Bacon Factory, which had invested much of the money required to build the railway. The line was also an essential link for service personnel stationed at RAF Compton Bassett and RAF Yatesbury during the Second World War.

The branch line was closed to all traffic on 18 September 1965 and the track was lifted in 1967.[168] The bridge itself was eventually removed in 1971, due to its decay leaving it too unsafe to use. A footbridge was installed here c2002, and is still known as the 'Black Bridge' by locals.

The field name of Sadlers Mead, may have come from the Sadler family. A Robert Sadler bequeathed the interest on £300, to buy 'drab clothes for women', his only condition being that 'his own tomb was always kept in repair.'[169]

Monkton Park School opened in 1968 at Sadlers Mead.

On the corner of Cocklebury Road and Sadlers Mead is a soon to be demolished part of Chippenham's educational history. Chippenham District County School was housed in this fine building from 1900. It became the Chippenham College of Further Education in 1948, and is now just a small part of Wiltshire College's Chippenham campus. **College Close** was named after its proximity in 1964, as was **Newall Tuck Road**. Edward Newall Tuck was headmaster of the school from 1896 to 1939. He was

The winter of 1962 to 1963. Eric Palmer skating on the River Avon. Monkton House can behind.
Photograph - Nicola Pithouse (daughter).

also a town councillor, and mayor of Chippenham in 1921 and 1931. He did much to advocate preservation of natural and historical features of Chippenham.

In 1956 two separate secondary modern schools were formed for boys and girls, with the boys staying at Cocklebury Road until 1959.

Gales Close is named after 'Gales Gift' which was bequeathed in Robert Gale's will dated 4 July 1612. After Gale died in 1628, the vintner from London left £20 a year to the the 'deserving poor' of the

---

[168] The Calne Branch, Tanner, 1972.

[169] Daniell, J.J., (1894), p. 165.

parish. After his wife Dorothy also died, these funds were distributed by the Bailiff and Burgesses 'To the poore of the Towne of Chippenhame on the ffeaste daie of St Thomas the Apostle. Also twenty shillings to the Preacher for his sermon and twenty to the Baillif for drinck'.[170]

Bruges Close is named after William Heald Ludlow-Bruges, who was chairman of the Wiltshire Quarter Sessions and Deputy Lieutenant for Wiltshire during the first half of the 19th century.

Many of the streets at Monkton Park are named after the former residents or owners of the old Monkton Estate.

Seymour Road is named after the Seymour family who held the manor between 1536 to 1686.

Bayliffes Close is named after William Bayliffe who rebuilt the Manor House at Monkton Park in the 1686.

Edridge Close and **Esmead** honour Esmead Edridge, who was the great grandson of William Bayliffe and inherited Monkton House in 1778.

Carrick Close is named after Carrick Moore, another former owner of Monkton House. Moore gave land at London Road for the Cottage Hospital in 1897 and his daughter Miss Mary Carrick Moore bequeathed £100 to its upkeep in 1925. She was the great niece of General Sir John Moore who died in 1809 whilst in command of the British Army at the battle of Corunna in Spain, during the Napoleonic war.[171]

Lady Coventry Road is named after Lady Muriel Coventry. Her husband bought the Monkton estate in 1919 from Miss Mary Carrick Moore. She was the last resident of the house before it was divided into flats.

Other street names in Monkton Park are;

---

[170] Goldney, F. H., (1889), p.

[171] Wiltshire Times, 25 April 1925.

Martins Close was presumably named after the Martin family, but no evidence of such has yet been discovered.

Montague Close Edward Montagu of Lackham House was MP for Chippenham from 1698 to 1700 and was the eldest son of James Montagu and Diana Hungerford.[172] The spelling used for the street name is the more common variation, so perhaps this was used either for simplicity or by mistake.

Villiers Close is named after the Villiers family, Earls of Anglesey, who held land in the area in the 17th century (See Anglesey Mead).

Wyndham Close is named after the Wyndham family of Allington, who were passed the estate there in 1749 (See Allington).

Darcy Close is named after Lord Darcy who possessed the rights to the market in Chippenham before selling them to the Sherrington family of Lacock. This street was one of the last to be built in Monkton Park.

---

[172] The History of Parliament: The House of Commons 1690-1715

6 - Langley & Greenways

Foundry Lane became the centre of the town's expanding industry, with businesses attracted to the area because of its proximity to the new railway station. However, the foundry which was established by William Eyres & Arthur Silcock c1832, was already here before the arrival of Brunel's Great Western Railway, as was the engine shop of Bayliss & Jones.
Rowland Brotherhood set up business in 1841 taking over the foundry c1845, and was awarded contracts by the Great Western Railway up until 1861. From then his company's closure in 1869, which was due to financial trouble, the iron foundry made parts for railways and bridges all over the British Empire, many of which were due to contracts given to him by his friend Isambard Kingdom Brunel. To keep up with demand, the foundry needed to be open day and night.
It's closure had a huge impact on Chippenham, as it employed c200 staff. The population of the town dropped between the 1861 and 1871 censuses due to its closure.[173]

Ron Blake working in Westinghouse in the 1960s. Photograph - Ginny Wilkins (daughter).

Later, part of the works were used by James Bakewell Warrilow for the production of his 'fine flintlock guns', and in 1890 was took on by the Wiltshire Bacon Curing Company.
It reputedly became the 'largest bacon factory in England' at the time. The bacon factory closed after a fire in 1987, and the company merged with Harris' of Calne, which then became part of Bowyers of Trowbridge, eventually closing itself in 2008.

George Hathaway was a 'white' cooper, who came to Chippenham from Slimbridge in 1869. He established a butter churn works at the old timber yard of Mr Dixon opposite Lansdowne Place, London Road. Shortly after he moved to a more spacious site on the corner of Old Road and Foundry Lane, previously part of the works used by

---

[173] Leleux, S., (1965),

Rowland Brotherhood.[174] This piece of land, was originally a field called 'The Wall Ground'. Hathaway's successful butter churn business remained here from 1869 to 1934, during which time his churns became famous throughout the world, winning many awards.

His son Nicholas Hathaway was a mechanic who customised imported French cars in part of the factory. This venture was interrupted during the First World War when munitions were produced instead.

The requirement for butter churns declined in the 1930s when new manufacturing techniques were introduced. Hathaway tried to keep the factory alive by switching to carpet sweeper production, but this was unsuccessful and the company ceased operations in 1937.

Now the various factories which covered this side of Foundry Lane are long gone, and the land is home to Hathaway Retail Park, which opened in 1990.

George Hathaway at 32 New Road. Photograph - Peter Hayes (great grandson).

Langley Road is the road to Langley Burrell, its parish boundary extending into Chippenham before St Paul's church was built. The word *langley* comes from the Anglo Saxon *long lea* meaning *long pasture.*

This road follows the route of Maud Heath's Causeway, ending at the bottom of Langley Road by the Little George roundabout.

Maud Heath Court is a small modern development just off Langley Road which includes a veterinary surgery.

Maud Heath lived at Langley Burrell until her death in 1474. She bequeathed land and property to the care of trustees, the income of which, was to be be used to pay for a raised walkway into Chippenham through the areas which flooded.

At the end of Langley Road, a plaque is set in the boundary wall of the former Clift Hotel building, to mark the end of Maud Heaths Causeway. This marker post has not always stood here. At one time

---

[174] Wiltshire Times, 24 January 1931.

there was a stone pillar on a mound in St Paul's churchyard, but both of these are now gone. It is likely that this monument predates the building of the church and was moved out so not to take up valuable burial space in the churchyard.

In 1894, the Rev Daniell wrote about how the mound and pillar had 'both disappeared' and called it 'apathetic barbarism to subvert this ancient monument'.[175] The original stone inscription was moved over to the present position, but this too vanished, probably after road improvements made in 1893.

In 1968, when the new Barclays Bank was being built in the Shambles, the old stone inscription was discovered covering a drain in the cellar. It was presumably put there when the original bank was built in 1920.

This echoes a story from 1930, which was told by an elderly man named Chivers, who heard as a boy that the stone had been stolen by young men during the 1822 Langley Riot and was hidden in a cellar in the town![176]

This stone marks the end of Maud Heath's Causeway, and stands at the end of Langley Road opposite St Paul's Churchyard.

Joining Langley Road to Greenway Lane is **The Hamlet** which was previously known as *Ashe Cottages,* whilst it was part of the Scott-Ashe estate. When built, the houses were surrounded by fields, giving the feel of a small hamlet. It is a one way street due to the narrow width of the road. **Hamlet Court** is also here.

Just past the entrance to The Hamlet, on Langley Road, sits a line of 11 pairs of semi-detached houses built by Taylor, Woodrow & Company in 1937. These were twinned with another row of 14 pairs of semi-detached houses on Greenway Lane behind. *Carlton, Mayfair* and *Queenboro' Deluxe*, were among the names given to the style of houses, that were used to market the new development.

---

[175] Daniell, J.J, (1894), *p. 123*.

[176] Chamberlain, J.A., (1974), pp. 19-20.

The second and third pairs on Langley Road are marked as being 'reserved for cinema' on the builders plan. This may have been another site, along with that at New Road, which had been under consideration for a new cinema, before the Astoria was built a year later.[177]

Many homes in Chippenham have individual house names, some of which were named after a person or place connected with battles from the time they were built. Such examples in Sheldon Road include *Omdurman*, *Gordon* and *Khartoum*. **Tugela Road** was built around the time of the Boer War, and the Battle of Tugela Heights was a British victory of February 1900, which brought an end to the Siege of Ladysmith.
Local builder Frank Field, who was based on Malmesbury Road, built houses here in 1902. There there is a date stone with the inscription 'FF 1902' at number 47. Ernest Chequer had a motor car workshop in Tugela Road in 1903. During the Second World War air raid shelters were built here for the employees of Westinghouse.

Hawthorn Road is named after *The Hawthorns* which is a substantial property which had seven bedrooms and its own Brewhouse.[178] It was built by William 'Burt' Whitmarsh, who lived here until his death in 1880. Whitmarsh was the Coroner for North Wiltshire, and the father of ten children.[179]
In 1944, Cannings College took over the building as part of their private school network.[180]

Tugela Road, 1945. Photograph - John Tucker.

Hawthorn Road itself, along with its first 14 houses, were built in 1907 by Frank Fields.

Next along Langley road is **Wade Mews**, which is named after Chippenham Town Council Mace-Bearer William 'Bill' Wade. His son John, also held the role up until his death in 2002, one month before his father also passed away.

---

[177] G19/760/373, WSHC.

[178] Wiltshire Times & Trowbridge Advertiser, 16 October 1880.

[179] Taunton Courier & Western Advertiser, 23 March 1881.

[180] Wiltshire Times & Trowbridge Advertiser, 8 January 1944.

This small cul-de-sac backs onto the former Westinghouse site, where Bill had worked in the Drawing Office. Bill started his career with the RAF, retiring in 1957 when he joined Westinghouse. He carried on his association with the RAF as chairman of the RAFA. A prominent member of the community, he also was involved with Chippenham Sea Cadets for over 30 years and the Carnival committee for over 20 years. He escorted all the town mayors in office between 1980 and 1997, on official functions as mace-bearer. Chippenham Town Council presented him with the award of 'Honorary Townsman' in 1990, the same year he was given the British Empire Medal in the Queen's Birthday Honours List

Next is **Clift Avenue** which was built by Messrs Bush & Hudson c1936, originally comprising of just 23 three-bed semis, and eight 'lock-up' garages.[181] Named after 'The Clift' which was the drop from Old Road to New Road, now hidden by New Road's buildings.[182] A 'clift' means 'cliff'.

Chippenham Clift is recognised as being the end of Maud Heath's Causeway. Another theory is that the route of the causeway was changed when the Great Western Railway was built c1840, cutting through the main route into town. In the *Highways and Byways of Wiltshire*, G.H. William, suggested that the actual Clift was at the top of Monkton Hill. There is a more significant drop there, so the idea does hold some credence, especially when we know that the pillar marking the end of the Causeway, was moved more than once.

In 1850, Charles Bailey, surgeon, built his house called 'The Clift' on Langley Road. He was a charitable man. In 1855 he built six homes during 1855 at Foghamshire called 'Providence Place' (not to be mistaken for Providence Terrace), for destitute widows and the relatives of deceased doctors. This was part of his work for the Medical Benevolent Trust.[183]

Bailey was unmarried and was 'somewhat eccentric in his habits,' an example of such was that he kept his tailor made coffin in his possession throughout the ten years before he died.[184] Another, was his acquisition of a rare bird which was shot whilst it fished in the River Avon in the summer of 1833. The bird, which had a wing span

---

[181] G19/760/362, WSHC.

[182] Chamberlain, Joseph A, (1976), pp.9-10.

[183] Platts, Arnold, (1947), p.68.

[184] Bath Chronicle, 28 August 1873.

of four feet, was believed to be a species of Pelican.[185] Clift House was demolished in 1982. The name of Clift House is now given to the purpose-built development for the elderly which is on this site. Clift Cottage on the opposite side of Langley Road. It is a grade II listed 19th-century residence.

Evans Close and **O'Donnell Close** are named after the railway engineering works built in 1894 by Evans, O'Donnell & Co. Ltd. John Patrick O'Donnell and Arthur George Evans were producers of 'railway signalling apparatus'. The foundry of Foundry Lane, owned until 1894 by Jones & Bayliss, was acquired by the company. Some of the roller bearings made here were used on 'Big Ben' in London.

Clift Cottage on Langley Road is a Grade II listed building.

This company was sold to Saxby & Farmer in 1903, which were the inspiration for the names **Saxby Road** and **Farmer Close** on the 'Pew Hill Park Estate'. Saxby & Farmer were part of a merger in 1920 to form Westinghouse Brake & Saxby Signal Co Ltd. In 1982 Westinghouse became part of the Hawker-Siddley group.

This part of the town was, until 2018, dominated by the buildings of Westinghouse. They are now being slowly demolished to make way for a supermarket, hotel and housing. The large white concrete Westinghouse office building, which until recently was a landmark on entering the town by rail, was built in 1932, with an extra storey added in 1935. It has now gone, and will be missed by many who had fond memories of working there.

The ascent of Maud Heaths Causeway towards Langley Burrell is called **Pew Hill** and is home to Pew Hill House. A *pew* is another word for a 'sheepfold', which is an enclosure for keeping sheep. The existing Pew Hill house was built c1895 in the 'Maverick Tudor and Stuart' style by the architects Silcock & Reay of Bath, for a Miss Dickson.

An older Pew Hill house stood here, believed to have been built c1773, but this house was partially destroyed by fire on 22 January 1894. The decision was made to demolish and start over, rather

---

[185] Devizes & Wiltshire Gazette, 11 July 1833.

than try to rebuild. This older house was the home of Thomas Pocock c1851. Thomas was a woollen cloth manufacturer who ran Waterford Mills in Westmead Lane, employing at least 600 workers.[186]
The house was sold to Westinghouse on 6 September 1939, becoming their Head Office during the Second World War.[187] Later it was divided into flats for their employees, then a hostel for apprentices, until eventually it was used as the registered office of the company.

The current home of Chippenham Rugby Club is at Allington Fields, which can be seen whilst travelling along West Cepen Way towards the Bumpers Farm roundabout. Their previous home was at a recreation ground off Birch Grove. The only clues of this fact are in street names of the roads built over it. They were chosen by developer Heron Homes after completion c1991. They are **Twickenham Way, Lansdowne Grove, Lansdowne Court** and **Murrayfield**, home stadiums of England, Ireland and Scotland respectively.

Greenway Lane, **Greenway Avenue**, **Greenway Court**, **Greenway Park** all take their name from the original Greenway Lane Farm that was here before the houses were built. A small hamlet before the housing estate joined it to the rest of the town, it was recorded as the *Greenewaye* in 1605.[188]
Greenway Lane runs from Hill Corner Road to Malmesbury Road. Originally it would have joined Langley Road instead, but the building of St Paul's Church altered its original route onto its present course.
The Priory stands near this bend in the road and is a residential home for the elderly. Built in the early 20th century, it was part of the 'Arts and Crafts' movement, and is credited to Sir Harold Brakspear. On the other side of the road is the parish hall for St Paul's Church, a valuable resource used by many community groups. Sir Audley Neeld laid the foundation stone in 1917, and it was fortunate enough to recently receive a makeover in its centenary year.
At the other end of this road, Greenway Lane farmhouse still exists as a private residence called 'Greenways Grange'. This is all that

---

[186] 1851 census.

[187] Benson, 1982.

[188] Gover, J.E.B., (1939), p.106.

remains of the 17th-century farmstead. The surrounding farmland is now covered in 20th-century housing.

Greenways Business Park, which stands between Malmesbury Road and Hill Corner Road, was previously the home of Greenways maternity hospital. This fine Edwardian building was a private mansion residence built in 1900 by Captain Moubray Allfrey. It became a maternity hospital in 1948 but closed in 1988 when services were squeezed into St Andrew's hospital at Rowden Hill. Greenways was bought by developers, and despite every effort by English Heritage to have it placed on the listed buildings register, it was demolished to make way for the offices. Many townsfolk have fond memories of their stay at Greenways, and the hospital is often described as having a welcoming and 'homely atmosphere'.[189]

Greenways was the centre of new life in Chippenham for over forty years.

Ashfield Road - This is a combination of the family name of Ashe who owned much of the land in this area, and Frank Fields the builder, who lived on the adjacent Malmesbury Road.[190] There is a date stone on the Greenway Lane end of the street which informs us that these houses were built in 1904. The 'Malmesbury Road Estate' was built by Mr Fields on a field owned by Miss TE Ashe, and included nine houses fronting Malmesbury Road and both sides of Ashfield Road.[191]

Barrow Green - Barrow Farm is just north of the former hamlet of Hill Corner which gave its name to **Hill Corner Road**. This was the home of Robert de Hulle in 1333, so 'hill' may in fact be a corruption of *Hulle*. Barrow Farm was recorded as early as 1227 as *Barwe* which was probably derived from the Old English *bearu*, meaning *grove*.[192] Hill Corner is now part of the outer housing area in the north of the town, with the only indication of its former isolation being the age of the houses here compared to those surrounding.

---

[189] Domesday Reloaded, 1986.

[190] Barrett, G., & Jefferies, S., (1985), *100 Pictures of Chippenham Past.*

[191] G19/760/184, WSHC.

[192] Gover, J.E.B., (1939), pp.105-106.

Chandlers Mews - off Hill Corner Road is a development of 12 private dwellings built in 2017 by Cotswold Homes. A Chandler can be either someone who makes candles, or in this context, someone who deals in boats and boating supplies. Chandlers Mews was built on the site of a Boat Repair and Chandlery belonging to P&I Boats at Hillside Garage.

At the junction of Hill Corner Road and Greenway lane, there was an Italian prisoner of war camp. The soldiers were taken from here to St Mary's Church every Sunday for Mass. There is a plaque in the church porch made by the POWs as a thank you for the kindness shown to them, with the following inscription;

'Italian prisoners of the Second World War, would like to express their gratitude to the people of Chippenham for the humanity received during their imprisonment'.

Birds Marsh View faces the direction of the popular beauty spot Birds Marsh, a 59 acre wood that is a haven to wildlife that has been enjoyed by local people for generations. Since 2008 it has been under threat from nearby proposed housing developments, and now these plans are coming to fruition. Birds Marsh was called *Birch Marsh* as recently as 1840.[193]
In the summer months it becomes a 'labyrinth of evergreens, with gorgeous rhododendrons and a wealth of wild flowers'. According to Daniell, there used to be a breed of 'small yellow vipers' in the marsh, which were dangerous to the cattle feeding there. Birds Marsh was once part of the Langley Common estate, which was a free pasturage of 80 acres, given by Royal assent to the villagers of Langley Burrell and Chippenham. This changed however, when the demand for wool in the 16th century encouraged the reclaiming of enclosed wastes and commons by the nobility, which in turn drove out the peasantry.[194]

The new housing estate at Greenway Lane was built in 1938. Northwood, Oaklands, The Oaks, **The Orchids** (a later addition), Willow Grove, Birch Grove, **Broomfield**, Maple Way, Cedar Grove and Elmwood are all inspired by tree names.
The General Purposes Committee recommended the names Oaklands and Ashe Crescent for the new council estate at Greenway Lane in 1938. Edward Newall Tuck, who as well as a

---

[193] Platts, Arnold, (1947), p.89.

[194] Daniell, J.J., (1894), pp. 36-38.

councillor, was a representative of the Society for the Preservation of Rural England, asked that the names of the fields the new estates were built over, be retained. He produced a map from 1831 to show evidence of 'interesting field names' and also recommended that names of those who had helped improve the town also be used, suggesting as examples 'Keary' and 'Neale'. 'Keary Street' and 'Neale Crescent' were suggested but not adopted. Mr Vine pointed out the previous discussion of using tree names should be looked into (which was ultimately the decided theme). Mr Pannell thought that 'Westinghouse Crescent' should be used as the town 'owed a great deal to the company for its prosperity'. Although not adopted, the name would later inspire the naming of the development at Pew Hill House, and the Westinghouse name will actually now be used at the new estate under construction behind Park Avenue.

The names **Maple Way** and **Willow Grove** were both proposed by builder Bush & Hudson in 1938.[195] **Birch Grove** and **Elmwood** were recommended by the General Purposes Committee in the same year.[196] **Oaklands** and **Ashe Crescent** were also built in 1938. The small cul-de-sac of **Cedar Grove** off Elmwood was built much later, in 1959.[197]

Construction began on the 'Pew Hill Estate' c1951 with approximately 110 houses that were a mixture of 'Reema', 'Woolaway' and 'Traditional' type houses.[198]
A Tenants Association for the residents of the new estate at Barrow Green, Hill Rise and Northwood was formed in 1953. Its members sought the provision of a school and shops for the new estate.[199]
The Oaks became the new home of St Paul's Primary school in 1973, after the old school in Park Lane was demolished and the temporary annexe building at Broomfield was sold for housing. The Oaks consists of council flats built in 1965.[200]

---

[195] G19/100/10, p.261, WSHC.

[196] G19/100/10, p.220, WSHC.

[197] G19/100/18, p.76, WSHC.

[198] G19/700/24PC, WSHC.

[199] Wiltshire Times & Trowbridge Advertiser, 14 March 1953.

[200] G19/100/20, p.387, WSHC.

Heathfield, **Moorlands** and **Hill Rise** are all named after features of the landscape before it was covered in housing. The majority of the houses on these streets are of 'non-traditional' construction, such as the 'Woolaway' homes, which are a type of prefabricated building design that has long fallen out of favour with developers.
Heathfield was built for the council, partly on allotments, by Woolaway Contractors Ltd c1956. Moorlands was built later on the former Air Ministry Depot close by.[201]

The Ashe family owned much of the land on the Langley side of Chippenham, and **Ashe Close** and **Ashe Crescent** are both named after them. Notable Ashe family members include; John Ashe who was a leading Wiltshire clothier in the 17th century and the Rev Robert Martyn Ashe, a landowner who lived at Langley House in 1859 and a contemporary of the diarist Francis Kilvert.

---

[201] G19/723/10, WSHC .

7 - Hardenhuish

Originally a separate community in its own right, the parish of Hardenhuish slowly became part of Chippenham as housing spread outwards, officially joining in 1952. A settlement with Saxon origins, Hardenhuish was first mentioned in AD 854, as a manor being held by *Haregeard*. Archaeological evidence of Saxon dwellings were found here in 1977. Early variations of the name Hardenhuish include; *Heregeardinge hiwisce* in AD 854, *Hardenehus* in 1086, *Hardehiwis* in 1177. A *Hiwisc* is a family holding, so the name translates as the 'Home of Haregeard'. [202]

May Day celebrations at Hardenhuish Park c1908.

The modern houses at **Church View,** have the closest view of Hardenhuish parish church, which is dedicated to St Nicholas. This was built in 1779 using some of the stone reclaimed from an earlier medieval church it replaced further down the hill.[203] The parish register here survives from 1730.[204]
John Wood, the Elder, the famous architect of Bath was responsible for the church, with funding provided by Joseph Colborne of Hardenhuish. David Ricardo MP, the economist, is buried here (see Ricardo Road), along with John Thorpe MA, who was a 'distinguished antiquary' and author who died in 1792.[205]

The Old Rectory opposite the church, as the name suggests, used to be the home of the Rector the parish. In the middle of the 19th century the Reverend Robert Kilvert was appointed to this post. He is best known as the father of Francis Kilvert the celebrated diarist. As the parish only afforded a small income, Robert decided to open

---

[202] Gover, J.E.B., (1939), p.99.

[203] Griffiths, T.J., (1982),

[204] Kelly's Directory of Wiltshire 1915.

[205] Wiltshire Times, 6 February 1909.

a school in the Rectory, advertising as being 'for the sons of the gentry'. The school took on twelve boys aged 9 to 13 and was so popular that the children came from far and wide to attend.[206]

St Nicholas' Church stands close to the top of **Hardenhuish Lane**, which joins with the summit of Malmesbury Road in one direction, and leads down to the double-mini roundabout at **The Folly** in the other. The Folly's name does not come from the term used for an expensive or unpractical building, but either from 'fallow' meaning 'uncultivated land', or from *feuille* which translates as 'leafy', so it was possibly a wooded area at some point in the past.[207] The Folly also used to be known as 'Ferfoot Hill'.

Next to the Folly, **Old Hardenhuish Lane** finishes the original route of Hardenhush Lane itself. In 1966 it was proposed that this narrow residential road should be turned into a cul-de-sac, but this was not possible due to a covenant placed on the road when it was adopted by Wiltshire County Council. Instead a one way street was recommended, as is the case today.[208]

Hardenhuish House dates back to the late 18th century, though the manor itself is medieval. The grounds were purchased by the council in 1935 and used for housing and schools. The grammar school element at Cocklebury Road moved to Hardenhuish Park in 1939, due to overcrowding. A new secondary modern school for girls opened next to this in 1956, whilst another for boys opened further down the hill in 1959. In 1975, all three schools merged into two comprehensive schools. The grammar and the girls school became Hardenhuish School, whilst the boys became Sheldon School.

The school fields were used by US Army soldiers from the Armoured Division as a camp during the Second World War, with the officers headquartered at Lackham.

Portal Close - The last occupant of Hardenhuish House, whilst it was still a private residence, was Major Portal. Before this it was the home of the Clutterbuck family.

---

[206] Betty Coleman, (2014), *Buttercross Bulletin*, Chippenham Civic Society.

[207] Chamberlain, Joseph A, (1976), p.6.

[208] G19/100/21, p.338, WSHC.

Laines Head - The name derives from 'Poor Laines Coppice' which was still close by c1840. This was recorded as 'Layne Hills' in 1640. **Long Ridings** and **Ridings Mead** are both from field names, with **Brookwell Close** presumably also taking inspiration for its name from features of the landscape.

St Paul's Street is named after St Paul's church which was designed by the architect Sir George Gilbert Scott. A new church was needed when the Langley Burrell parish of St Peter grew with the increase of population, and the 'spiritual needs of the district around the railway station' needed to be met.[209] A chapel-of-ease in Chippenham was seen as the best solution, as the capacity for St Peter's in Langley Burrell was only 170, with only a small burial ground. An acre of 'glebe land' was chosen and the church was built at the cost of £4000. The consecration took place in 1854 with the Rev JE Jackson, Rector of Leigh Delamere, officiating the first service. According to Jackson, who was also a keen local historian, no new church had been built in the immediate neighbourhood for 700 years.

St Paul's Church looking from the corner of Malmesbury Road.

At the Marshfield Road end of the street, St Paul's House replaced three pairs of villas, reputedly built by Brunel for his staff during the construction of the Great Western Railway through the town.

Thurston Court is built on the old St Paul's School site at the corner of Park Lane and St Paul's Street. The school was here from 1857 to 1973 and was demolished in 1980, save for the Schoolmasters house, which can be seen on the corner, the date '1857' visible on the front.

---

[209] Platts, 1955.

Three times mayor of Chippenham Edward Thurston was the inspiration behind the name, as he was headmaster here between 1891 and 1925. He was held in high esteem by staff, pupils and ex-pupils alike, who presented him with a gold watch on his retirement. He was a 'conscientious school master and a loyal and devoted son to his aged mother', and never married but instead devoted his life to the service of others.[210] When he became mayor in 1925, the wife of the town clerk was chosen to act as mayoress.[211]

Class IV, St Paul's School c1909. Head Edward Thurston is on the far left.

St Paul's School was built on the site of a former 'Dame School' established on pasture land known as 'Home Ground' or 'Brook Ground.' This land was given by the Rev Robert Martin on 12 January 1857 and the school was formally opened on 6 April 1858.

Park Lane was previously 'Little George Lane' until it was widened and renamed in 1893. When St Paul's school was built it in 1857, it was known simply as 'Parish Road'.

The original Little George Inn was destroyed by a fire on 20 December 1903. The Turner family who lived and worked in the pub, were rescued thanks to the quick actions of Thomas Hathaway, of Chippenham Fire Brigade.

A stable lad, Herbert Banks aged 13, lost his life despite the best efforts of Thomas to save him. Mrs Turner, the Landlady, was woken by the smell of the fire and managed to rouse her husband. The staircase was alight so they had to escape through a window. The origin of the fire was never discovered.

The Little George was rebuilt in 1905 including the rear stables. These were demolished in 1970 to make way for the short link road between Park Lane and New Road.

The earliest record of the Little George Inn is on Powell's map of 1784. It is likely that the Little George was named after Prince George, the son of George III. This is supported by the fact that at that time there was a pub in the High Street called The George Hotel, which was known by the locals as 'Big George'.[212]

---

[210] Wiltshire Times & Trowbridge Advertiser, 1 August 1925.

[211] Wiltshire Times, 14 November 1925.

[212] Don Little, Chippenham Civic Society, 2009.

An early mention of the Little George occurs in antiquarian John Britton's childhood recollections c1779, in which he notes that it was a 'house famed for its strong fine beer'.[213] Although the building is no longer used as a pub, **Little George Mead** serves as a reminder of its past.

In 1822, the 'Little George Toll' was built opposite the pub on land used for part of St Paul's churchyard after it was pulled down in 1854. The toll was moved to Langley Common on land given by Rev Ashe opposite the junction with Hill Corner Road.

Park Terrace and **Parkfields** were constructed on a nearby part of the Hardenhuish estate parkland in 1905.

John Coles Park during an unknown event. Photograph - Jean Morrison.

John Coles Park is named after John Coles the chemist, grocer and wine merchant. He was born in Frome, but lived and kept shop in the Market Place. Coles was mayor of Chippenham in 1891, 1898 and 1914. When he died in 1916, he left £4000 in his will for 'the cultural and educational advancement of the people of Chippenham'. With this gift, the council repaid the loans taken out to purchase parkland from the Hardenhuish Estate.

The 15 acre park opened on 23 May 1923, complete with a bandstand built at a cost of £267 designed by Mr AE Adams. This was restored in 1987, and is still put to good use by the town band and visiting groups.

The first park-keeper, Mr Cue, lived in one of the two council houses at the main entrance to the park on Park Lane.

On opening day both the bowling green and the tennis courts were not ready to be used as the grass had not grown sufficiently.

On the 1923 ordnance survey map, the park is merely described as a 'recreation ground' and shows few defining features. Plans to build new houses on the 'Brookfield Estate' were submitted by Walter Rudman shortly before the park opened. A slightly scaled down version was built on the allotment gardens adjoining the 'new park', called **Parkside**.[214]

---

[213] Baines, Richard, (2009), p.145.

[214] G19/760/134, WSHC.

Parklands is a 1960s development of, and on land surrounding, the Gothic Revival style St Paul's Rectory, which was the work of Sir George Gilbert Scott. This mixture of sheltered and social housing became derelict by 2010. Now Parklands is being redeveloped, hopefully in a way that complements the Grade II listed rectory and its proximity to John Coles park.

John Coles Park, 1965. Thank you to Christine Toombs for this photograph of her youngest brother enjoying the playground.

Fleet Road is the main access road to John Coles Park. A furlong of land called 'the Fleete' was conveyed to William Newman, vicar of Chippenham in 1369.[215] In 1892, the two fields opposite the former St Paul's school on Park Lane, were called 'the Fleet'. This then became known as the 'Fleet Recreation Ground' and may have been used by the pupils of St Paul's School, The land was purchased from Canon Charles Griffiths by Edward Downing Rudman in 1919 and became the entrance to John Coles Park in 1923.

Off Fleet Road, towards the bowls club, is a short street called **Ricardo Road**. Born in Holland in 1771, David Ricardo was an internationally recognised economist who was the first to propose the control of money supply and credit. He also was a successful stockbroker making his fortune by the age of 25. In 1817 he published *Principle of Political Economy and Taxation*.

An old style blue street name sign for Fleet Road.

Although Ricardo was born Jewish, he married a Quaker and then later became a Unitarian. He died in 1823 at Gatcomb Park in Gloucestershire, but was brought back to Chippenham and was buried in St Nicholas Churchyard at Hardenhuish. Ricardo's grave is marked by a grand tomb designed by William Pitts, and is now a Grade II* listed monument. It is made of limestone ashlar and

---

[215] Daniell, J.J., (1894), p.150.

marble in the 'Greek Revival' style and includes 'naked hermaphrodite weepers'.[216] In an entry in Francis Kilvert's diary of 1874, it is claimed that his tomb cost £2000 to build.[217]
Captain Daniel Hugh Clutterbuck was the grandson of David Ricardo. The Clutterbuck family were well respected in North Wiltshire, with many family members holding prominent positions in society. Daniel was magistrate for Chippenham, was involved in local politics and had a career in finance. Primarily though, he was a military man, and was best known for serving with the 8th Hussars during the Crimean War. He returned as one of the 'Heroes of Balaclava', who had took part in the famous 'Charge of the Light Brigade'. In the years that followed, Captain Clutterbuck would regularly attend annual 'Balaclava Banquets' in London.[218]

A terrace of houses runs between Park Lane and Marshfield Road called **Springfield Buildings**. This was built by local builder John Henry Smith and was named after Springfield Farm which was close by at that time. An inscription on the side of the end house facing Park Lane, 'JHS 1853', confirms the builder and year of construction. These houses are only accessible by a small footpath. 'Springfield Place' is also here at numbers 5 to 9, along 'Prospect Place' at numbers 11 to 13, Park Lane.

The area at the western end of **Marshfield Road** was known as Landsend as early as 1820, but this name since fell out of use. It is still, however, recorded on the exterior of 52 Marshfield Road, with the inscription 'Landsend Place'. This is the end property of a fine terrace of houses built by Rowland Brotherhood for the employees of his foundry.

Number 52 Landsend Place, Marshfield Road.

Also in Marshfield Road, is the Astoria cinema built by William Henry Watkins. Opening in May 1939, this was meant to be much larger with a restaurant. In 1967 it was divided to allow for a Bingo hall on the lower floor, and then in 1973 the remaining screen was divided so two films could run at the

---

[216] www.britishlistedbuildings.co.uk

[217] Chamberlain, Joseph A, (1976), pp.10-11.

[218] Wiltshire Times, 30 October 1875.

same time. The Astoria was originally part of a chain owned by Emmanuel Harris. It is now part of Reel Cinemas who have invested in its future with an impressive refurbishment that is currently underway, that when complete, will provide five screens and other improvements.

The staff of the Astoria Cinema, Christmas, 1955. Photograph - Ann Brinkworth.

Opposite the cinema, stood the Order of St Joseph of Annecy Convent, now 11-12 Marshfield Road. It was known at the time as 'Suffolk Villa', and was used by the nuns for a relatively short period from 1866 to 1884. After arriving in Britain from India in 1864, the nuns made it their new home and mission, for Catholicism had not grown in Chippenham since the easing of laws against Catholics. The convent was run by Elizabeth Twomey, the former teacher at the chapel, who became known as Sister Josephine after taking holy orders. A school of twenty pupils were taught here in 1875, and included catechism classes for adults. There were four nuns listed in residence here on the 1881 census, three of whom were Irish and one French. After the convent closed and the nuns moved to Malmesbury, there would be no Catholic school in the town until 1938.

The large and imposing Bewley House was built on Marshfield Road in c1967, as the offices for the Chippenham & Rural District Council. The architect was Mr AD Kirby of the Wyvern Design Group.[219] The building was named after the original Bewley House that was demolished along with Great Western Hotel, which has been built here to serve those working on the railway close by.

Bewley House under construction. Photograph - Norman Tapp (taken by his brother David).

Western Villas were opposite until they were demolished in 1972, for the Department of Work & Pensions office. A stay of execution was given after an application to replace them with a three storey office block was turned down. The plans by Western Industrial Developments Ltd were possibly not radical enough, as this would have been much less imposing than the

---

[219] Pevsner, N., (1975), p.173.

tower block that was built in the end.[220] Western Villas were built by Brunel for employees working on the new railway line. Only a monkey puzzle tree still survives.

Western Arches from St Paul Street, c1972. Photograph - Robin Hardie.

Bristol Road runs from the end of Marshfield Road to the Bumpers Farm roundabout, where it connects with the rest of the A420 to Bristol.
The first turning past Landsend on this road is **Oak Lodge Close**. An elderly residential care home built in 1966 and Oak Lodge House are here.[221]

After Woodlands Road, the next turning on this side, is for **Park Avenue**. Colbournes Estates Ltd were responsible for this cul-de-sac of 72 houses, which in 1935 when the plans were put forward, were known collectively as the 'Hardenhuish Estate'. At this stage it was to be called 'Park Road', but this was changed to Park Avenue in 1936.[222] The original proposals included a second access from Bristol Road, joining on the second bend where number 32 is today, but the County Surveyor deemed this unnecessary.[223] The road remained as a cul-de-sac until recently, as it now gives access to a new housing estate built by Linden Homes on the former Westinghouse Sports Ground site. The new streets here highlight the town's connection with the railway, using the names; **Signal Way**, **Flying Scotsman Close** and **Westinghouse Park**.

Cricketers at Westinghouse Sports ground, 1960s. John (Harold) Summers is second from right in the back row. Photograph - Jean Summers (daughter).

The name 'Hardenhuish Estate' was used again, for another development opposite Oak Lodge House. Building began in 1937 by EH Bradley & Sons, with 22 houses on the entrance road of

---

[220] G19/100/21, p.9, WSHC.

[221] G19/100/21, p.303, WSHC.

[222] G19/100/10, p.16, WSHC.

[223] G19/760/338, WSHC.

87

Hardenhuish Avenue and the start of **King Alfred Street**.[224] Bradley's had wanted to call King Alfred Street 'Show Road' and Hardenhuish Avenue 'Okus Road'. Okus is a suburb of Swindon where Bradley and Son were headquartered. Both of these names were opposed by the Housing Committee, who had put forward the names 'Bradley Road' and 'Harnish Avenue'. Councillor Tuck strongly opposed that spelling of Hardenhuish, and also to the naming of a road after a developer. Upon his suggestion, it was agreed that Alfred Street and Hardenhuish Avenue would be best, although concerns by Councillor Dann over the vagueness of Alfred Street were later readdressed and 'King' was added.[225]

The new Linden Homes development off Park Avenue nears completion.

In AD 853, Ethelswitha the older sister of Alfred married the King of Mercia in the parish church at Chippenham where St Andrew's now stands. It is believed that Alfred himself kept a hunting lodge in the vicinity of the former Goldiggers site at Timber Street. King Alfred was forced to flee Chippenham for the Isle of Altheney after the Danes attacked Chippenham in AD 878. Later, to prepare for the counter attack, Alfred reconnoitred the Danes' camp personally whilst in disguise as a minstrel. With men from Somerset, Wiltshire and Hampshire he defeated the Danes at Ethandune, stormed the stockade at Chippenham and forced Guthrum to surrender.[226]

This theme is continued with nearby **Wedmore Avenue.** The Treaty of Wedmore was made between Guthrum and Alfred in AD 878 and was concluded at Chippenham. By this treaty, the Danes agreed to accept Christianity and leave Wessex.
Wedmore Avenue was originally a cul-de-sac, but was joined to Malmesbury Road in 1949 to create another access point to the estate.[227]

---

[224] G19/100/10, p.162, WSHC.

[225] Wiltshire Times, 11 September 1937.

[226] Crick, J., & Van Houts, E., (2011), p.406.

[227] G19/760/397, WSHC.

Yewstock Crescent is named after 'Yewstock', which was a hamlet just north of here on the road from Chippenham towards Malmesbury. It was recorded as 'Yeo stock' in 1840.[228] As part of the Hardenhuish Estate, public events used to be held here before the housing estate was built. These included the Chippenham Flower Show and the Chippenham Horse Show.
In 1939 it was split into two streets due to difficulties with numbering. The names were 'Yewstock Crescent East' and 'Yewstock Crescent West'.[229]

In AD 866, the Danes led by Hungar and Hubba invaded the east coast of England. Hungerford hosted a battle between Hungar and the Saxons, hence the origin of the name.[230] This served as a preamble to events involving King Alfred in Chippenham. Therefore, **Hungerford Road** was chosen as a suitable name following the theme on the estate. Also strongly connected to the history of the town, is the Hungerford family. The Hungerfords were lords of the Hundred of Chippenham until Walter Hungerford was accused of high treason during the reign on Henry VIII. He reputedly called the King a 'heretic' and enabled William Byrd, vicar of Bradford of Avon, to experiment with alchemy in order to see into the King's future. For these acts, William had his head chopped off on Tower Hill, and all his lands were confiscated by the Crown.[231] The Hungerford family remained an important part of Chippenham life however. Edward Hungerford was MP for Chippenham in 1621.

This house on Malmesbury Road was originally a lodge for Hardenhuish House.

The original plan for this estate, detailed King Alfred Street as a through road linking up with East Yewstock Crescent, removing the requirement of Hungerford Road and Wedmore Avenue altogether.

---

[228] Gover, J.E.B., (1939), p.99.

[229] G19/100/10, p.349, WSHC.

[230] Jackson, J.E., (1856), p.6.

[231] Daniell, J.J., (1894), pp.59-60.

The central 'circus', or turning area, would have been accessed directly opposite Hardenhuish Avenue.[232]

Malmesbury Road is so named, simply because it is the road to Malmesbury. Equally simple is the naming of the small cul-de-sac **Milestone Way**, which is a mile from the town centre in the direction of Malmesbury. The old milestone still stands close by, outside what was the King Alfred Public House.

Malmesbury Road. Postcard sent in 1906.

Opposite John Coles Park and off Malmesbury Road, **Deansway** was originally a cul-de-sac rather than the through road it is today. In 1985, a Neolithic leaf-shaped arrowhead was discovered in the garden of number 35. The Deansway development, began in 1934 by Downing & Rudman, consisting of 'labour saving' homes with an asking price of £600.

At the top of Malmesbury Road, past the traffic lights and opposite the footpath to Birds Marsh, are the last houses on leaving Chippenham. These four pairs of semi-detached homes were built c1935 by Downing & Rudman and were separated from an earlier group by a private road belonging to Mr H Brinkworth.[233]

---

[232] G19/760/380, WSHC.

[233] G3/760/859, WSHC.

8 - Woodlands and Audley

Woodlands became part of Chippenham when the borough was extended in 1914, originally being part of Hardenhuish Parish. There is a small wood that exists today in Woodlands. It is a small patch of land at the corner of **Woodlands Road** and **Bristol Road**. Hardenhuish brook cuts through and this area is a mini haven for wildlife. The name Woodlands however, derives from a family name rather than a natural feature. Walter de la Wudelande of 1289 is the earliest recorded, and others of significance include; Richard Wodelonde who was one of the original trustees for Maud Heath's gift. Leonard Woodland who was Bailiff in 1578, John Woodlande also Bayliffe in 1626 and 1635. Also, in 1618, Richard Woodlande left £5 in his will to be used for year long loans to town residents.[234] The earliest houses here were built at 'The Woodlands' c1900 by Downing & Rudman in a terrace on the western side of the road.[235]

Hardenhuish Brook trickles through the copse at the Bristol Road end of Woodlands Road. Unofficially called 'Woody Woods'.

Another interesting feature of this street is the Church of the Good Shepherd, which was opposite the turning for Canterbury Street. This spot is now the home of the Chippenham & District Royal Antediluvian Order of Buffaloes.

Also, there are the **Woodlands Bungalows** which can be found tucked behind the main terraces further along on the western side of the street.

Two residents of Chippenham, Thomas Henry Davison and his wife Mary, were passengers on the ill-fated maiden voyage of the RMS Titanic. Born in 1880, Thomas (known as Harry) was the blacksmith

---

[234] Gover, J.E.B., (1939), p.92.

[235] G3/760/76, WSHC.

son of Thomas Cook Henry Davison, a corn Miller, and Sarah Ann Long of Sheldon Road. He was living at Woodlands Road when he married Mary Elizabeth Finkenagel of Malmesbury in 1902. After, the couple resided at 32 Marshfield Road following a brief stay in Cleveland, Ohio in 1908 which was were Mary's family were from. They decided to return to America to settle in Bedford, Ohio, but postponed their departure so they could 'enjoy the novelty' of crossing on the famous ship. They bought 3rd Class tickets in 'steerage' for £16 2s and boarded at Southampton on 10 April 1912.[236]
Thomas was woken when the ship hit the iceberg, dressed to see what had happened, then returned to wake his wife. She survived, but Thomas was lost, his body never found or identified.

Former model village on the corner of Woodlands Road opposite Marlborough Court. Photograph courtesy of Mark Coath-Wilson.

Plantation Road can be found off Woodlands Road. A 'plantation' refers to an area of artificially grown trees for a variety of purposes, including for timber production. Also here, **Beechwood Road** and **Chestnut Road**, are also named after types of trees.
The estate was built in 1938 by Beard & Son of Swindon, partly on land which was formerly the location of 'Woodlands Grove', the home ground of Chippenham Rovers Football Club. Rovers resigned from the Wiltshire Football League in 1937 when their ground was sold for housing. Dr JH Nixon of Oakleigh, club president, resigned due to health reasons and only a handful of members turned up for the AGM. The lack of interest and the loss of their home ground led to the decision to seek an amalgamation, and by 1960 one was completed with Corsham Football Club. The Grandstand was sold for £22 10s. Originally the estate was planned as being much bigger with an additional street called 'Alder Road', and Plantation Road was to extend through to Brook Street in plans resurrected in 1947, which

VE Day party at Chestnut Road, May 1945. Photograph - Ruth Gilhooly

---

[236] Behe, G., (2012).

would have included the land used for Redlands School and St Clements Court.[237]

Sheldon Road is named after the manor of Sheldon. The name comes from *Scylf dun* which translates as the 'place on the hill'.[238] Sheldon road originally ran all the way to Sheldon Manor, but the rest of this route is now called Frogwell. Other variations of the spelling of Sheldon have included; *Shuldon* in 1287, *Sholdon* in 1308, *Shulden* in 1417 and *Shildene* in 1428.[239] The medieval settlement of Sheldon no longer exists, and it is thought this was because the plague left the village uninhabited in the 16th century.

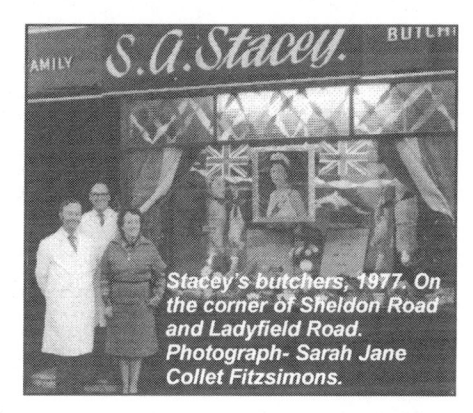

Stacey's butchers, 1977. On the corner of Sheldon Road and Ladyfield Road. Photograph- Sarah Jane Collet Fitzsimons.

Sheldon Manor House was built in the 13th century and claims to be the oldest inhabited manor house in Wiltshire. Scenes from the re-boot of the BBC historical drama *Poldark* were filmed at Sheldon Manor.

Nearby is the 'Holy Well', also known as the 'Star-well' because of the star shaped fossils that can be found there. This natural spring is in the middle of a field on Stowell Farm and still has the ruins of a stone structure around it. The 17th-century antiquarian John Aubrey recommended taking the water with a 'syrup of violettes' and had been informed that the water was 'good for the eies'.[240] The work of Aubrey has been invaluable to historians of

Sheldon Road including the Methodist Church. Postcard sent in 1905.

---

[237] G19/760/393, WSHC.

[238] Chamberlain, Joseph A, (1976), p.6.

[239] Gover, J.E.B., (1939), p.91.

[240] Daniell, J.J., (1894), p.33.

Chippenham, as he was the earliest collector of information relating to the antiquities of Wiltshire.[241]

In 1937 a new public house was built on Sheldon Road to help serve the expanding population to the west of the town. The final incarnation of the Five Alls was designed by Walter Rudman and Mr W Cockram, and came complete with a skittle alley and garden. It was built for George's Bristol Brewery at a cost of £7,000.[242]

Also on Sheldon Road is the 'Nursery Estate' built by Morris & Jacombs of Birmingham in 1964. They had put forward the names 'Nursery Close', 'Nursery Court' and 'Nursery End' for consideration. The council did not think any of these were suitable and recommended **Stonelea Close**.[243] This, and the later addition of **Andrews Close** built by Wilcon Homes in 1982, was built on land previously used by Chapel Nurseries.

Westminster Gardens is a relatively modern development with a name that compliments neighbouring **Parliament Street**. The UK Parliament is of course, situated in Westminster, London. Parliament Street was built by Messers Downing and Rudman who were responsible for many local streets and buildings. Westminster Gardens is built on land which used to be Lowden Nursery.

Audley Road was previously known as 'Gastons Lane', a name which continues in usage in **Gastons Road**. This is an old local name which derives from Richard atte Gerston of 1299, who owned a farm which later became known as 'Gastons Farm'.[244] Gastons Lane is recorded as 'Gasson's Lane' in 1900. A field which ran the length of where Audley Road was built called 'Great Gastons', was here until it was sold for housing in 1907.[245]

---

[241] Platts, Arnold, (1947), p.85

[242] Western Daily Press, 5 March 1937.

[243] G19/100/20, p.340, WSHC.

[244] Gover, J.E.B., (1939), p.92.

[245] Wiltshire Times, 24 August 1907.

The houses in Gastons Road were built by Walter Rudman c1934, along with numbers 1 to 10 Woodlands Road behind. These became part of the 'Wessex Estate'.[246]

Audley Road along with **Dallas Road** and **Neeld Crescent**, are named in honour of Sir Audley Dallas Neeld who was the Baronet of Grittleton, MP and mayor of Chippenham. Dallas Road was proposed in 1923 by the 'Neeld Trustees' to be built on land held by them.[247] Houses were eventually built here c1937 in the typical style of the period with gabled roofs and bay windows.
The Fire Brigade moved into a new Fire Station built at Dallas Road in 1945, with a upgraded version built later on the same site in 1974.

The end of Audley Road where it meets Marshfield Road was, until very recently, the West End Club but has now been turned into a gym. Next to the former club is a couple of shop units, which at one time was home of the Excel Fish and Chip Shop. Just past this is the new 'Audley Mill' development, which has been given the name of **West End Close**. Next is **Hardbrook Court**, a much larger block of flats. Around the bend, **Seagers Court** was built in 2010 and named after Seagers Coaches which had their depot here. These flats are opposite Hardbrook Court next to the turning for Gastons Road.

Canterbury Street was constructed by Messrs Downing and Rudman, whose work had a significant impact on the town, having been responsible for many buildings. It was named after the London address of Saxby and Farmer's head office at Canterbury Road in Kilburn.
Downing Street was chosen by the building company in memory of Simon Downing who started the business in 1830. He had the honour of being the last person to be buried in St Andrew's

A street sign forms part of a doorway in Canterbury Street.

---

[246] G19/760/286, WSHC.

[247] G19/100/7, p.476, WSHC.

churchyard. In 1866, Annie, the only daughter of Simon Downing married Edwin Rudman at St Paul's Church.[248]
The firm became Downing, Rudman & Bent when Edward Bent bought it in 1936. Its new headquarters at **Spanbourn Avenue** were completed the following year and this site was used to build **Rudman Park** c2007.
Downing, Rudman & Bent were responsible for post-war projects including the Bridge Centre and the NAAFI building in Wood Lane. They were also known for wood carvings, and were often contracted to carry out restoration work, most notably at Battle Abbey.

Churchward Court is on the corner of Lowden Avenue. This was named after George Jackson Churchward CBE, who was Chief Mechanical Engineer of the Great Western Railway at Swindon. George was also a trustee of the GWR Medical Fund Society before he died in 1933.

This brick has been used to decorate the front wall of a garden in Hungerdown Lane.

Cinders End is a small cul-de-sac off **Lowden Avenue**. The 'Cinder Path' was the name given to the right of way which ran across the former Lowden Brickworks site. The Lowden Syndicate Ltd of Audley Road produced bricks which they advertised as 'hand made, sand faced, red face bricks of attractive colour and true in shape' and 'wire-cut bricks of best quality, sound and true in shape and colour'
Romano-British pottery sherds dated from between AD 43 and AD 409, were found in one of the clay pits in the 1960s.
Both Churchward Court and Cinders End were built c1993 on the former 'Teachers' Centre' owned by Wiltshire Council.

Gabriel Mews and **Goldney Avenue** are named after Sir Gabriel Goldney MP The Prince of Wales (later King Edward VII), personally invested Gabriel as 'Grand Senior Warden' of the Prince of Wales' Lodge of Freemasons. Gabriel worked as a Solicitor and owned property in Chippenham and Corsham, where the Goldney family held the title of 'Lord of the Rectory'.
His eldest son was Sir Prior Goldney. Prior lived at Derriads and was a Major in the Royal Wiltshire Yeomanry. His second son, Frederick Hastings Goldney, was believed to be the oldest Freemason in the world until he died in 1940 aged 94. The Goldney estate passed to Frederick when Prior died in 1925. Frederick

---

[248] Devizes & Wiltshire Gazette, 7 June 1866.

served Chippenham as Conservative councillor, mayor and was also the High Sheriff of Wiltshire. He was a founder member of the Sunningdale Golf Club and was often spotted driving around the town in his vintage Maudsley car. Frederick was also a writer. His works included *Freemasonry in Wiltshire* and *Records of Chippenham*, which has proved extremely useful during the research for this book![249]

Castle Combe and Chippenham Dairy Milkmen with their fleet of electric milk floats c1960. Photograph - Trisha Lewis.

An ancestor, also called Gabriel Goldney, in his will of 1681, charged £6 a year on his land at Tytherton to provide coats for 'six honest labourers'.[250] These were distributed at Christmas time to those considered the most deserving. The coats were made by a Chippenham tailor with a different design each year. **Farnewell Close** also has a connection to the Goldney family. Henry Farnewell was the first bailiff of the town following the grant of a charter from Queen Mary in 1554. Farnewell was an alias of the Goldney.

Chris Eels, proudly standing at the front of his dairy's new premises in Goldney Avenue c1960. Sadly he died in 1965 aged only 50. Photograph - Trisha Lewis (daughter).

Wholesale and retail grocers Messrs William Kingham and Sons Ltd were on Audley road where **Kingham Close** is now. This company was based in Farnham, Surrey with sites at Reading and Banbury in addition to the one at Chippenham. Kingham's became part of the Oriel Food Group, which later merged, as part of Argyll Foods, into Safeway PLC.

The name **Loyalty Street** comes from the town motto 'Unity and Loyalty' which is displayed under the Borough coat of arms.

---

[249] Bath Chronicle and Herald, 24 February 1940.

[250] Daniell, J.J., (1894), p.163.

In December 1937, four English oak trees were planted along the edge of the Loyalty Street children's playground, with Mayor Culverwell officiating. The trees were meant to act as a permanent commemoration of the coronation of King George VI. When planted, the trees stood about 12 feet tall, and would be of substantial size if they were still there today.[251] This was not to be, because in 1992, **Sidney Wood Court** was built on the play area. Sidney Herbert Wood was a former member of Chippenham Council. He died suddenly in 1972 aged 65, after twenty years of 'conscientious and diligent service.'

VE Day street party at Loyalty Street playground. Photograph - Angela Reynolds.

Phipps Court is built on the site of Phipps' shop formerly at 15 Loyalty Street. This was a grocery store ran by Leslie and Janette Phipps since the 1960's.

Marlborough Court was built on the site of Lowden school, after it moved to Lords Mead in 1973 and became St Peters Church of England School. The original railings can still be found on the Sheldon Road side.

The decision behind choosing the name of **Dover Street** remains a mystery, but it appears that it was decided when the original building plans were amended. Fewer homes were meant to be built here, but more were squeezed in, most likely under the instruction of the council. The houses were built primarily with concrete by Edwin H. Bradley and Son in 1936 as part of a wider existing housing scheme. The Dover Street houses were part of a group of 44 covering a four and a half acre site including the eastern end of Canterbury Street and bordering Audley Road. The plans highlighted the 'rather better class of property on the plots fronting Audley Road' which were to go on sale for £495 each.[252]

Marshall Street is named after Alderman Lionel Hasler Marshall who was mayor in 1897 and 1908. During his time in office Marshall contributed to the mayoral ceremonial garments by donating a hat. Lionel was County Secretary of the Royal English Arboricultural Society, and as a surveyor by trade, a member of the Surveyor Institution. He was also the First Commandant of the Chippenham

---

[251] Western Daily Press, 30 December 1937.

[252] G19/760/341, WSHC.

Voluntary Aid Detachment based at the Neeld Hall during the First World War.

Lowden School celebrates the Coronation of King George VI in 1937. Photograph - Lyn Jones Campbell

In 1911, land was purchased by William Henry Palmer of Bridgwater for the purpose of building a new housing estate. **Palmer street** was central to the plan drawn up in 1907, documented in the sale papers. A terrace of houses were already situated on the north side of the road.

Unity Street runs parallel to Palmer Street, and is the 'Unity' to the 'Loyalty' in the town's motto. According to the plans, Unity Street was originally meant to be called 'Osborne Terrace'. There was also plans for a small street called Madeline Road on the other side of Ladyfield Road.[253]

---

[253] G19/150/3, WSHC.

9 - Lowden and Rowden

Just before the road through Lowden winds under the small railway tunnel, **Utterson View** is tucked away. Elizabeth Utterson left money in her will to build almshouses for poor elderly women of the town. These are still used for charitable purposes today, and can be found next to the New Testament Church of God. This was formerly St Peter's Church, designed by Graham Awdry and dedicated in 1886.
St Peter's moved to Lords Mead in 1968 to serve the expanding west side of Chippenham.
In St Andrew's church, a stained glass window was given by Elizabeth Utterson in memorial to her husband James, who died shortly before her, in 1884.[254] James Utterson was the registrar for births and deaths, and also an Insurance agent for London Corporation Fire & Life, both of which he administered from his office on the Causeway.

Towards the Bath Road end of Lowden is **St Peter's Close**, which serves as a reminder of the church. The land here was used as part of the Condensery Piggeries and later a Nursery. The houses were built between 1967 and 1975, with the first group by Wilson's of Swindon.[255] Mr Peter Snape was responsible for the more recent properties, which he began to build behind

Two views of Lowden village from the railway embankment. Utterson's Almhouses are to the right of St Peters Church. Both postcards sent in 1905.

Chequer's Yard in 1974.[256]

---

[254] Daniell, J.J., (1894), p.184.

[255] G19/100/22, p.149, WSHC.

[256] G19/100/25, pp. 628-629, WSHC.

On 24 August 1855, a Methodist chapel opened in the then small hamlet of Lowden. To mark the occasion, the new congregation and others carried out a singing procession to Ivy Park. This had been kindly lent for the day and a huge tent for up to 600 persons was erected. The chapel was possible due to the generous donations of land by Mr JB Dowding and 5,000 bricks from Mr Rixson.[257] Although no longer in use for this purpose, the structure is still part of the Chequer's Yard buildings. The chapel was equipped with a day school for children up to ten years old. It was acquired in 1905 at a cost of £40, for use as a reading room for the young men of the area.

St Margaret's School, Rowden Hill c1960. Photograph - Deborah Garland.

St Margaret's Gardens is a small cul-de-sac built on land which had belonged to St Margaret's Roman Catholic Convent.

The SMG sisters were invited to come to Chippenham to open a convent home for elderly sisters which would be dedicated to St Anne. SMG is an initialism for the 'Poor Servants of the Mother of God' who are based in Roehampton.

Mr Cullen's house on Rowden Hill was purchased to establish the convent and the sisters were warmly welcomed at the train station on 7 October 1937.

As the first mass was said on the feast day of St Margaret Mary, the Bishop suggested that the convent should be named St Margaret's rather than St Anne's.[258]

On the 1939 register, six Nuns are listed as being in residence. Ellen Dowling was the Mother Superior with the other five listed as teachers.

Parts of the original convent buildings still survive as St Mary's Roman Catholic Primary School which opened in 1959, with

Frank 'Pop' Tarrant, landlord of the Plough Inn. The family goose, 'Lucy', has just laid an egg at the age of 19. Photograph - Caroline Saye (granddaughter).

---

[257] The Primitive Methodist Magazine, vol.34, p.623.

[258] Coggles, J. & N., (1998).

Tollgate Cottage, Lowden Hill. Most of property is an extension of the original toll house built in 1835.

additions made in 1962. There was also an independent fee-paying school called St Margaret's in the convent, from 1955 to 1968.
The last of the nuns, Sister Mary, left Chippenham in 2003 to support the mission in Kitui, Kenya, but the school is still owned by the SMG order.

Lowden was formerly a manor, the earliest record of which was 1258 when Henry III gave the land to William de Valeree, the Earl of Pembroke.

Pavely Close is named after the Pavely family of Westbury, who were next to be granted the Manor of Lowden. They sold it to the Gascelyn family of Sheldon Manor in 1272.[259]

Now the name of a road, **Lowden** then became the name of a village that was separate from the town of Chippenham. It was first recorded in 1249 as 'Lolledon' and later in 1494 as 'Loldon', and it is thought that the name comes from 'Lolla's Hill'.[260]

Lowden Hill was 'Lowden Green' in 1742 and 'Lowden Lane' on Powell's map of 1784. It was part of the original route to Bath before Bath Road was built.[261]

Opposite Chequer's Yard, just past the bottom of St Mary's School playing field, is **The Quadrangle**, a narrow private road leading to what was formerly known as 'The Piggeries' due to the type of farming that was carried out there and in the surrounding area. The shape and layout of the buildings forms a courtyard which is otherwise known as a quadrangle. Over on Chequer's Yard, stood the Plough Inn, where a 'Pig Club' was held. These were common during the 1940s and 1950s due to rationing, as people were encouraged to be as self-sufficient as possible. The significant dip

---

[259] Platts, Arnold, (1947), p.6.

[260] Chamberlain, Joseph A, (1976), p.5.

[261] White, George A.H., (1924), p.12.

that The Quadrangle sits in may be explained by the fact that at one time this area was used as a clay pit. The clay was excavated and transported by donkey and cart to the Lowden Brick Works off Audley Road. Many of the red coloured bricks produced there were used by the Lowden Syndicate Ltd to build houses in Dallas Road, Lowden Avenue and Audley Road. The brickworks closed in 1936 and the site was used for military exercises during the Second World War.[262]

'Brooklands' was the name given to the development of the first 44 homes built at Rowden. This first phase was only granted permission after Redcliffe Homes won a lengthy battle in the Court of Appeal. A street called **Brooklands** was added later as the first built here was given the name **Coppice Close**. Brooklands was inspired by the proximity of Ladyfield Brook. Coppice Close is a reminder of 'Rowden Down Coppice' which was one of the Borough lands here given by the Crown in 1554.

Rowden Lane is named after the manor of Rowden and means 'Rough down' or 'Rough Hill'.[263] The 'Rowden Manor Drive' development was the second phase of building work by Redcliffe Homes .

Legend has it that Sir Walter Hungerford 'the spendthrift' staked the manor during a game of bowls, infamously calling out 'here goes Rowden' on his last chance.[264]

During the Civil War, Sir Edward Hungerford of Rowden House was a supporter of Parliament. Both he, and Sir Edward Baynton of Bromham, were hostile to the Crown.

The manor house was described by Aubrey as a 'large, well built, gothic house, with a court within, a fair hall very well furnished with armour, and a moat about it'.

This all changed after the siege here during February 1645. The '400 horse and foot' besieged by c4000 Royalists, surrendered after enduring extreme cold and hunger. The 'mansion' was 'rifled and fired' by the victors, yet some buildings remained habitable even if on a much smaller scale. The foundations and moat of this once great house are still traceable, and burnt stones have been found in the garden walls.[265]

---

[262] Jefferies, S., (1987), p.76.

[263] Gover, J.E.B., (1939), p.91.

[264] White, George A.H., (1924), p.4.

[265] Daniell, J.J, (1870), pp.8-9.

A cannon-ball from this period was discovered at Rowden Farm and given to the town council as a gift in 1950.[266]

Milbourne Way is another of the new streets. It is named after Milbourne Farm which was nearby at Patterdown. The main buildings of the farm have now been divided by the road to Lacock.

The new Eddie Cochran memorial, Rowden Hill.

Cochran Avenue is named in memory of American rock 'n roll singer Eddie Cochran, who was tragically killed after his car crashed into a 'lamp standard' on Rowden Hill. The accident happened on 17 April 1960, whilst Cochran was travelling with fellow star Gene Vincent and friend Shelly Sharon, who were both injured when they were thrown from the car. Cochran and Vincent had been performing in Bristol at the end of a twelve week tour of the U.K. and were on route to London Airport to catch a flight to Los Angeles. Cochran's injuries were severe and he died aged 21 on Easter Sunday in St Martin's Hospital, Bath.

There is a memorial for Cochran at St Martin's which had become rather worse for wear, so in September 2018 it was replaced with a more substantial structure.[267] Led by Adam Gittings, the Eddie Cochran Memorial Project brought the community together, as well as Cochran fans from further afield, to raise money for the memorial. An example of the positive use of social media.

Close to where the railway line crosses Bath Road, is a small cul-de-sac called **Brunel Court**, which was built c1988. Brunel spent time in Chippenham during the construction of the Great Western Railway, staying at Orwell House with Rowland Brotherhood. His works office still exists in the train station car park, and shows the style used for the original station build. During a stay in 1841, Brunel

---

[266] Wiltshire Times, 11 March 1950.

[267] The Stage and Television Today, 21 April 1960.

had to leave Chippenham unexpectedly when news reached him of a serious fire in the timber yard of the Bristol & Exeter Railway Company at Temple Meads. If it wasn't for his quick organisational actions, the whole railway terminus could have been destroyed.[268]

Opposite Brunel Court, on the corner of Patterdown, stood the west gate toll house which was built by Chippenham mason John Woodman c1834. On the 1851 census, the toll collector is listed as Thomas Hornsey, a Chelsea Pensioner. Along with the other tolls, this was closed in 1870 and reverted to a private residence. Unfortunately it was badly damaged after a lorry crashed into it in 1965 and had to be demolished.

Rowden Road leading to; **Burleaze** was pasture land which belonged to the Borough of Chippenham. In an update to the Borough Charter by James I in 1604, the borough was granted permission to keep twenty sheep at Burleaze. In 1658, the bailiffs let the land to Richard Stevens for six years at a rental of £6.
The name Burleaze comes from *bur*, which is a corruption of borough, and *leaze* which means pasture or meadow.

The Ivy Field Housing Estate was built on a large part of the former Ivy Estate. Entry to the estate is by **Charter Road**, which then leads through to **Royal Close**, both of which are named after the Royal Charter given to the town on 2 May 1554 by Queen Mary.[269] The charter was later surrendered to King

The Ivy Fields c1915. This was part of the Ivy Estate, which is now covered in houses.

Charles II in 1684, but restored by King James II in 1685. James passed through the town in 1687, probably using the opportunity to grant the Charter officially in person.[270] The Charter made the bailiff second in rank only to the King himself within the manor, as he was commissioned to protect Royal interests.[271]
Also on the estate is **Field View**, consisting of flats which have a commanding view of what is left of Ivy Fields. Recent work has

---

[268] Bristol Mercury, 1 May 1841.

[269] Platts, Arnold, (1947), p.9.

[270] Daniell, J.J., (1894), p.62.

[271] Daniell, J.J., (1894), pp.56-57.

created the Ivy Wildlife Garden at Royal Close which has improved the appearance of this formerly neglected area. The idea was thought up by Terry Carr. He started the project in April 2014 with Jen and Deyck Hanchett, who are fellow local residents. They have had support from the GreenSquare Group and funding from the Wiltshire Wildlife Trust.[272]

Gypsey Lane is an old 'right of way' which links Bath Road to a small modern group of homes called **The Cloisters**, and continues as a single track road to a waterworks. Planning permission was granted to build a new Police station on land here in 1949. At this time the Police station was in Park Lane and would eventually move to the former NAAFI building in Wood Lane. This is now empty as they are using part of the Wiltshire Council building in Monkton Hill. Eventually permission was rescinded in 1953 by the Ministry of Housing and local government who refused to support the compulsory purchase order. The two acres chosen was valuable farming land belonging to the Ivy Estate and in use by a tenant farmer, who had objected due to most of his other land being susceptible to flooding.[273]

The Erleigh Drive estate was built c1987 by Sinclair Homes and is made up of detached homes with generous gardens. The streets here are named after the families who owned Rowden Manor in medieval times. First, **Erleigh Drive** which is named after Sir John Erleigh who was lord of the manor from 1392 to 1434. Margaret Erleigh, John's daughter and heir, married Sir Walter Sandes and the manor passed to his family, **Sandes Close** is named for this reason. **Maur Close** records when Lady Agnes St Maur widow of Godfrey St Maur was granted Rowden by Henry III in 1250. After which she became known as Agnes de Rouden.

An interesting man-made feature in the grounds of Lowden Manor is Primrose Hill. This is a small circular hill with steps to the top, surrounded by trees. It can be seen from the footpath in Erleigh Drive.
Built a few years after the Erleigh Drive estate, the houses at **Tall Trees** have a commanding view of some rather tall trees at the Ivy, some of which were imported from North America. Also, the Ivy Estate orchard stood on the opposite side of the road. The many impressive mature trees in this area probably date back to when the

---

[272] Chippenham Civic Society bulletin.

[273] Wiltshire Times, 7 March 1953.

footbridge and estate gardens were still in existence. A green 'Chinese' footbridge used to cross the road here just before the turn. Built by Mr Norris who lived on land at the Ivy. It was taken down when the estate was broken up in a sale in 1869, and the road was widened. Local legend was that the ghost of a White Lady haunted this spot.[274]

'Tall Trees' overlooks the imported North American trees of the former Ivy Estate

Rowden Hill was previously just called 'Rowden' until the name change in 1939.[275]

There once was an annatto factory at 'a mansion at Rowden Hill' c1860s to 1900. It was began by a chemist called William Nicholls, and continued after his death in 1870.[276]

It is likely that this was at the magnificent 'Rowden Hill House' next to the Hospital, which was formerly the Wiltshire Area Health Authority Headquarters. It was built c1860s in an 'eclectic style, mostly classical with some rundbogen (round arch) details'.[277] It is now boarded up and faces an uncertain future.

Annatto comes from the seeds of the Achiote shrub which is native to South America. It is used to give colour to dairy products, and can be seen as the orange skin on some types of cheese.[278] The fluid extract of annatto was first manufactured by Nicholls in order to colour cheese and by 1860 it was 'almost universally used for that purpose'.[279] His success was helped by his presence at the Great Exhibition of 1851, where he offered samples of his 'Beaufort Hunt Sauce', alongside showcasing his fluid extract of annatto.

At the top of Rowden Hill, the land opposite St Mary's School which includes the roads mentioned below, was also part of the estate owned by the SMG Catholic Order. This land was offered to the

---

[274] White, George A.H., (1924), p.12.

[275] G19/100/10, p.313, WSHC.

[276] Wiltshire Times, 24 January 1931.

[277] www.britishlistedbuildings.co.uk

[278] www.wshc.eu

[279] The Farmer's Magazine,1860, volume 17, p.295.

council for purchase in 1973, but they declined as a previous attempt with a housing application in 1968 was refused, meaning they would be unable to use the land for council housing.[280] This former ownership and proximity to an existing Roman Catholic establishment would have been the main influence behind the choice of street names here.

St Francis Avenue leads up to the hospital which opened in 1947. It was originally built as Chippenham Union Workhouse in 1858. Much of the original buildings still survive and are still in use. The workhouse had its own vocational school, teaching c60 to 70 children from when it first opened.

St Francis helped the sick and the poor. The current Pope chose Francis as his Papal name, because he also wished to concentrate on helping those in the greatest need. A good choice for a street with workhouse and hospital connection

The name of **St Luke's Drive** was probably chosen here because St Luke, who was a physician, is the patron saint of physicians and surgeons. Therefore, it is an ideal name for the access road to the hospital and a doctors surgery that are situated opposite a Roman Catholic primary school. Further along Bath Road, coming down Rowden Hill towards town is **St Teresa's Drive**. St Teresa is the patron saint of sickness, particularly headaches, so this appears to follow the same theme.

St Joseph's Drive is next to the Catholic school and appears to follow the same saintly theme.

---

[280] G19/100/25, p.440, WSHC.

10 - Hungerdown and Ladyfield

The field name of 'Hungerdown' is given to **Hungerdown Lane**, and refers to the poor quality of soil for growing crops. Part of this area was used by the Air Ministry for 100 houses. They were built by Messrs A Hanson & Sons Ltd for £42,637 on behalf on the council, for the civilian workers brought in for war work at RAF Hullavington in 1939.[281] At this time there were c250 people on the housing waiting list and there was concern that those who already worked in the borough would be made to wait longer.

The Kingfisher public house was built on Hungerdown Lane c1962 by Wadsworth brewery. This upset may people because of the 'beautiful, red brick farmhouse' which was demolished to make way for it.[282] A small supermarket was built in 1968 further along on the same side. This was a Gateway until 1989 then Somerfield. Now the building is home to a charitable furniture recycling centre called 'Waste Not Want Not' and the 'Classic Wok' Chinese takeaway.

Chippenham Hospital still makes good use of some of the original workhouse buildings.

In the late 1960s, land was secured on Hungerdown Lane for a larger Catholic Church and a secondary school. In 1970, the plans to build the school on were still on the table, and trees were felled in preparation for the sale of the land. However, the idea was dropped as the Catholic Diocese decided that it was not a good idea to pursue the project.[283]

---

[281] Western Daily Press, 9 February 1939.

[282] Catherine Brown & Phyllis Craddick, Chippenham Street Names Facebook page.

[283] Coggles, J. & N., (1998).

In 1954, the Hopgood family secured land on the corner of Ladyfield Road and Hungerdown Lane for an independent church. Former Plymouth Bretheren originally from London, they broke away from the church and came to Chippenham start their own. The prefab church lasted here for 29 years before the building was replaced in 1996 and again in 2009.

Hungerdown Lane was upgraded to an A-road in 1965 becoming part of the A350. Many local residents opposed this and the higher speed limit that came with it. West Cepen Way relief road was built in the late 1990s and the traffic reduced along with the speed limit.

Local residents protest against the speed limit on Hungerdown Lane, which was the A350 until Cepen Way opened.

The Pheasant public house is on the corner of Hungerdown Lane, and was originally called the 'New Inn'. Close by was the 'New Inn Toll Bar', where on the 1851 census, Anne Church was listed as the toll collector. The 'toll bar' would have been a simple wooden booth rather than a toll house, which explains why we cannot see evidence of it today.

Both **Orchard Crescent** and **Orchard Road** were built on allotment gardens and a nursery in which fruit trees used to grow.

The **Ladyfield Road** housing estate was first planned in 1908, but the first homes weren't completed until c1914. These were designed by William Robert Osbourne, who was a student of Sir Harold Brakspear. In March 1922, a further 42 'workmen's dwellings' on a plot of land adjoining the Ladyfield estate, had been completed by Mr Rudman. The rates for council tenants at this time started from 9 shillings a week.

The more modern development of **Little Down** was built partly on allotments off Ladyfield Road backing on to Parliament Street, and a former residence called 'The Bungalow'.

When **Kingsley Road** was first built in the 1939, it was originally a small 'close'. It was much later c1992, when the rest of the road was added on the adjacent playing fields.

Kingsley Road Community hall was built in 1998 as a new home for Sheldon Road Playgroup at a cost of £120,000. Local companies and charities formed a partnership to fund the project. Prangle & Carey donated £9,000 and carried out excavations at a reduced price, Wavin donated the plastics and Downing, Rudman & Bent built the structure free of charge. The Chippenham Borough Lands Charity gave £50,000.[284]

Famous novelist Charles Kingsley once mentioned 'pretty Chippenham' in one of his books, but it is unclear if he was the inspiration for this particular street name .

Lackham Circus is named after nearby Lackham. 'Circus' in this context means a round open space near a street junction, and is from the Latin word for circle. It was completed as part of the 'Hungerdown Building Estate', along with Kingsley Road, in 1939.[285]

In February 1943, plans were drawn up for a temporary housing scheme off Hungerdown Lane. This consisted of two and three bedroomed bungalows, to house some of the families from the blitzed Bristol area. Broadmead, Fishponds, Filton Way, Portway, Ashton Road and Southmead were the names of streets that made up the Prefab estate. These names were chosen as a comfort to the new residents, as they were 'named after areas that the people had come from.'[286]

These were gradually replaced in the 1960s. Many former residents can recall the poor conditions they had to endure in these 'Bungalows'. In some cases they were so damp anything put in the airing cupboard would go mouldy.[287] During the winter, ice could be found on the inside of windows and 'wallpaper used to glisten with the frost'.[288] It was particularly bad during the winter of 1962 to 1963 when the

Kingsley Road c1975. Photograph of, and supplied by, Jean Cook (Wilkins).

---

[284] Kingsley Road Community Hall page.

[285] G19/100/10, p.349, WSHC.

[286] Chamberlain, Joseph A., (1976), p.122.

[287] Julie Barry, Chippenham Street Names Facebook page.

[288] John Archard, Chippenham Street Names Facebook page.

3 Kingsley Road. L-R: Patricia Bishop, Maureen Major, ?, Marjorie Hornigold, Teresa Major, ?, William Hornigold, Alison Major. Photograph - Jean Cook.

country was buried under snow for three months. As they were single storey, 'snowdrifts completely covered the windows'.[289] There were ingenious methods used to combat the cold, which included taking a 'heated brick to bed wrapped in a blanket'.[290] For some, the bungalows 'felt like paradise' compared to their previous accommodation following the Second World War. The conditions at the displaced persons camps were even more basic.[291]

The names of **Southmead** and **Portway** were kept when permanent housing gradually began to replace the Bungalows from 1961 onwards, although not in the same exact locations which they are in now. **Stockwood Road** was added and all the other names discarded. Two further names were also adopted; **Chelwood Road** and **Westerleigh Close**.

Westcroft - Forty-two 'non-traditional' bungalows and 20 houses were built here in 1970 to replace the 46 individual aluminium bungalows built c. 1947. This was to increase the living capacity on the estate from 138 to 284 people.[292] The earlier Westcroft housing scheme, was entered along with the Derriads scheme, into the Ministry of Health Regional competition for the 'best designed housing' estate in 1950.[293] Behind these, where a playing field is now, a quarry used to be in operation, which may explain why this has remained free of housing.

Broadmead c1950. Photograph - Val Badder.

---

[289] Lin Walsh, Chippenham Street Names Facebook page.

[290] Ruth Griffin, Chippenham Street Names Facebook page.

[291] Victor Mandryko, Chippenham Street Names Facebook page.

[292] G19/100/23, p.17, WSHC.

[293] Wiltshire Times, 11 March 1950.

At the far end of Westcroft is a small road leading to the North Wiltshire Bowls Club called **Litherland Close.** This is named after bowls champion and former club director Mel Litherland of Chestnut Grange, Corsham. Mel sadly died in 2008 so the development, which was built by Westlea Housing, was named in his honour to recognise the contribution he made to the club. A ceremony confirming this decision was held on 4 March 2009.

Brook Street takes its name from Ladyfield Brook which runs underneath and alongside the road. It was a replacement for Kingswood Avenue when the prefab bungalows were demolished to enable the construction the 'Brook Street Estate'. This consisted of a large number of properties which included houses, flats and bungalows built here between 1962 and 1967.

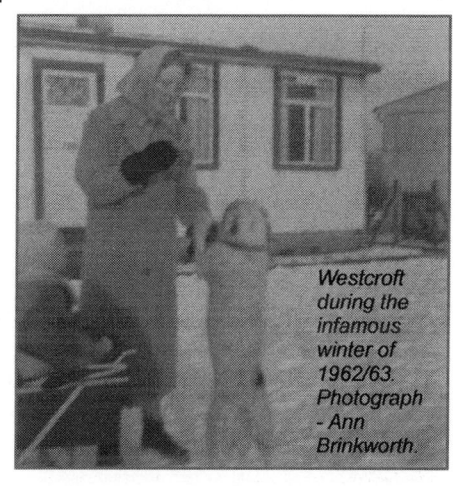

Westcroft during the infamous winter of 1962/63. Photograph - Ann Brinkworth.

Phase one was started in 1962, with properties on Wessex Road, Honeybrook Close and the southern section of Saxon Street.[294] **Saxon Street** reminds us that the first significant settlement at Chippenham was in the Saxon period around AD 600. **Wessex Road**, which was later accompanied by **Wessex Close**, refers to the name given to the region of the country controlled by the Saxons. Both Saxon Street and Wessex Road were previously part of Clifton Road, which carried on through to where **Clifton Close** is now, meeting up with Redlands near **Patchway**.

In 1962, the names of Saxon Street, Wessex Road and Honeybrook Close were chosen by the council out of a number of suggestions put forward by school children. Pupils at the grammar school, the secondary modern for boys and the secondary modern for girls, were invited to enter a competition. The three successful suggestions were made by Susan Walker, Marian Phillips and Susan Rowley from the girls' school. Each were presented with a £1 voucher by the mayor.[295]

---

[294] G19/723/12, WSHC.

[295] G19/100/19, pp 347,359, WSHC.

Honeybrook Close has Ladyfield Brook running next to it before it passes under Hungerdown Lane. There is a Honeybrook Farm at Biddestone which has been designated a 'Site of Special Scientific Interest' by English Nature. This is due to the 'undisturbed meandering stretch' of the Bybrook river and other natural features here that are 'rarely found in lowland Britain'.[296] Sadly, 97% of lowland meadows like the one at Honeybrook, have disappeared since 1945.[297]

Also on this estate is **Neeld Crescent** which is named after the Neeld family of Grittleton. Neeld Crescent, along with homes behind on the southern side of Brook Street, those at the entrance to Saxon Street and the group in Redlands facing the triangular green, was phase two of the Brook Street Estate, and was began in 1964 by Messrs Clark Bros of Swindon.[298]

Stapleton Road was the original name of the link road from Redlands to Brook street, which skirts the triangular green area mentioned above.

Swain family outside their 'Bungalow' in Keynsham Road, c1946. Photo courtesy of Roger Swain.

Keynsham Road and Leigh Wood ran parallel with each other between Redlands shops and what is now Brook Street. These streets spanned an area which is now a large green area, with a footpath. This area became a popular space for children to play, despite the council's efforts to prevent them from doing so. Their idea was to landscape it in such a way that ball games could not be played there, presumably in a similar manner to the field behind Kingsley Road. A campaign by residents, aided by the local paper, put a stop to the plans.

At the top of Keynsham Road

---

[296] Natural England Website.

[297] Farmers Weekly, 30 June 2000.

[298] G19/723/14, WSHC.

was Sutton's shop, a favourite place for the local children to buy sweets which would have still been 'on ration'.
The Head Postmaster wished for a sub-post office to be provided in the 'Folly' area, so land adjoining Sutton's was earmarked for this purpose in 1962.[299] Later, the new rank of shops included 'Folly Stores' under the running of Mr PM Sutton and Mr V Beasley.[300]

The construction of phase three of the 'Brook Street Estate' began with Redlands, Clifton Close, houses on the northern side of Brook Street and Boothmead in 1966. Plans for phase three comprised of housing for 484 people across a 12 acre site. Second World War bungalows were demolished to make way for these.[301]

Redland shops including the Post Office. The first shop here was Sutton's Stores.

Patchway (1967) and Redlands school (1973) had not yet been built.
Boothmead was originally part of a through road to **Redlands** called Horfield Road.
The land on which **Applewood Road** was built was owned by E.W. Beard, builders of Swindon, who had already worked on Plantation Road and Beechwood Road behind. This was originally planned as a continuation of the 'Plantation Road Estate'. Plans from 1937 and a revision from 1947, show the intention to join Plantation Road to Brook Street and build homes on the land which Redlands School has occupied since 1973.[302] Instead, the Brook Street end of Beard's land remained empty, and was used by local children as an unofficial playground until Beard built a smaller development of just nine traditional family homes c1984.[303] By that time, **St Clement's Court** and its elderly sheltered accommodation had already been built on the part of this land nearest Woodlands Road, in 1976.

---

[299] G19/100/19, p.253, WSHC.

[300] G19/100/25, p.489, WSHC.

[301] G19/700/25PC, WSHC.

[302] G19/760/393, WSHC.

[303] Applewood Road sales brochure c.1984, supplied by Marian Jones.

11 - Queens Crescent & Cepen Park South

The **Queens Crescent** housing estate was built in stages between 1963 and 1984 by developers Laing and Smith & Lacey. It was intended to be a mixture of privately owned and council homes. The building began in 1963, in the northern section bordered by Derriads Lane and Hungerdown Lane. Queens Crescent, Spinney Close, The Firs, Clover Dean and Fairfoot Close were all named in 1966 as the first part of the 'Derriads Park' or 'Derriads Farm Estate'.[304]

Fairfoot Close - The origin of this name is unclear, but could be a corruption of 'Ferfoot', as in the nearby Ferfoot House off Bristol Road. This was built c1890 as the home of the Hathaway family, and is now an elderly residential care home.

The gap between Hungerdown Lane and the houses in Fairfoot Close can be explained by the fact that a large pond was here and although now filled in, may not have been considered suitable for building on.

Clover Dean is a descriptive name, the 'dean' more commonly spelt 'dene' (as found in Rumble Dene). A dean in this context, comes from *denu* meaning 'valley'.

Spinney Close is also a descriptive name, with 'spinney' being another name for a small area of trees and bushes, often planted as a shelter of game birds.

Some of the original trees which used to border the football ground can still be seen in the Queens Crescent estate.

The land at **The Firs** was the home of Chippenham United Football Club from 1947 to 1962. Before the Second World War the two main football clubs in the town were Chippenham United and Chippenham Rovers. Rovers played at a ground close to Town's over on what is now Plantation Road just of Woodlands Road. They disbanded in the early 1960s when they amalgamated with Corsham FC

---

[304] G19/100/21, p.207, WSHC.

Chippenham Town were established in 1875 and are still going today.

In the 1950s, the combined matchday support for the three clubs was often 2,000 or more, which considering the population of Chippenham at the time, was quite considerable and shows the interest in football was strong. Local businessmen Mr Townsend even had to close early on Saturdays so that his staff could attend matches!

United were formed with the aim of achieving more success through professionalisation. Town were not keen on going fully professional, instead taking the semi-professional option, so did not take up an offered position in the highly rated 'Wiltshire League'.

In August 1947, permission was given by the council for a change of use of the land at Hungerdown Lane. By 1948, the ground had shelter for up to 800 supporters and dressing rooms built. The pitch was fully enclosed by a steel fence and plans were on the table to increase covered areas for up to 3,000 including some seating.

The Firs was a military storage depot during the Second World War. The surface was flattened by moving the topsoil to either end of the site, which had created a kind of natural bank behind each goal.[305] There is still a line of trees that borders where the football ground was situated.

The first match between Town and United was a reserve game at Hardenhuish Park in 1949. This attracted 2,300 spectators, but later that season the record attendance for a game in the town was achieved for another meeting between the two sides. The figure of 4800 is still the Town's record for a football match.

There was much friendly rivalry between United and Town, with one common prank played by the United fans, was to plant a small fir tree on the centre spot on the pitch at Hardenhuish Park the night before a fixture. United had become known as The Firs after the name of their home.

United's demise was due to financial troubles. Ideas suggested to help included twice weekly greyhound racing, but their application to the council was refused when lodged in 1959. In the end public

---

[305] Twydell, D., (1986), pp 62-95.

apathy was blamed when the club finished in 1962 and permission was quickly sought and granted for housing at the Firs.
The next phase of the Derriads Farm Estate development began in 1968.[306]

The street names of **Cranwell Close** and **Trenchard Close** serve as a reminder of the temporary RAF homes which were built here in 1939.

The next part of the estate was built c1968. The streets are named after cathedrals and other popular tourist destinations.

Minster Way - A Minster is a church of significant importance, usually a cathedral.
Ripon Close - Ripon Cathedral in North Yorkshire
Coniston Road - Lake District village National Trust.
Wells Close - Wells Cathedral in Somerset.
York Close - York Cathedral, otherwise known as York Minster.
Kent Close - Known as the 'Garden of England'.
Silbury Close - Silbury Hill close to Avebury.

Also part of the 1968 group, **Kilverts Close** is named after the diarist Francis Kilvert, who lived at the parsonage at Kington Langley. Kilvert left us entertaining and often comical writings on his daily life whilst living in the area. He was born at Hardenhuish Rectory in 1840.

The streets to the western side of Queens Crescent were built by Smith & Lacy c1970. They are named after castles.

Arundel Close - Arundel Castle in West Sussex.
Berkeley Close - Berkeley Castle in Gloucestershire.
Carnarvon Close - Carnarvon Castle in North Wales.
Wardour Road - Wardour Castle in Wiltshire.
Windsor Close - The Royal residence of Windsor Castle.
Farleigh Close - Farleigh Hungerford Castle in Somerset.
Conway Road - Conway Castle in Wales.
Sarum Road - Sarum Castle near Salisbury in Wiltshire.

Queens Crescent Primary School was built at Windsor Close c1996.

---

[306] G19/100/22, p.241, WSHC.

More cathedral themed street were added c1973.

Winchester Close - Winchester Cathedral. Off Sarum Road, and
Salisbury Close - Salisbury Cathedral in Wiltshire. Off Coniston Road. Both were built by Smith & Lacy.[307]
Gloucester Close - Gloucester Cathedral in Gloucestershire
Truro Walk - Truro Cathedral in Cornwall

The final part of the estate was built c1983, with the streets named after Wiltshire country houses.

Avebury Road - Grade I listed manor house. Also, William de Avebury was the first recorded vicar of Chippenham. He held the position during the reign of Henry III.[308]
Littlecote Road - Grade I listed Littlecote House at Chilton Foliat near the eastern border of Wiltshire.
Wardour Road - The 18th-century Palladian 'New Wardour Castle' was the seat of the Arundell at Wardour near Tisbury.
Lydiard Road - Grade I listed Lydiard House at Lydiard Tregoze near Swindon.

Cepen Park South

All of the streets in Cepen Park South are named after UK racecourses. The land sold for housing and the Sainsbury supermarket (opened 9 August 1990) was farmland owned by the King family. They had successfully kept and trained race horses, and asked that as a condition of the sale, this would be remembered in the names of the streets.

A Mr GA King is recorded as living at Camp Farm off Hungerdown Lane in 1928.

The house at Camp Farm was originally designed by architect John Birch for Mr RP Long. Birch's design was awarded a medal by the Royal Society of Architects. In 1971, the land surrounding Camp Farm was owned by Builders Smith and Lacy.[309] Later, the farm was owned by Francis King, and his brother Frederick ran Derriads Farm.

---

[307] G19/100/25, p.463, WSHC

[308] Daniell, J.J., (1894), p.149.

[309] London Gazette, 21 January 1971.

Residents from the past and present have fond memories of the fields and seeing the horses that used to live and train here. It appears that the King family may have been quite successful at horse training. This land is remembered as 'the farm that trained racehorses, 'Sporting King' and 'King of Sport".[310]

Horse racing is not often thought of with Chippenham in mind but it was popular here at one time. In the early 19th century, horse races were held in Chippenham itself. These 'very popular' events took place on a mile long course at Westmead c1815.

After the supermarket, the first street to be built was **Ascot Close**, and it was here that the first homeowners moved in.

The houses and accompanying streets were built by Barrett, Wimpey and David Wilson Homes. As promised, the following names chosen are all of racecourses. No further explanation or description is required;

Aintree Drive, Ayr Close, Beverley Close, Brighton Way, Catterick Close, Cheltenham Drive, Chepstow Close, Chester Way, Devon Close, Doncaster Close, Epsom Close, Exeter Close, Folkestone Close, Goodwood Way, Hamilton Drive, Haydock Close, Hereford Close, Hexham Close, Huntingdon Way, Kelso Court, Kempton Park Court, Lingfield Close, Newbury Drive, Newmarket Close, Newton Abbott Close, Plumpton Close, Sandown Drive, Sedgefield Way, Southwell Close, Taunton Close, Thirsk Close, Towcaster Close, Warwick Close, Wetherby Close, Wolverton Close.

John Belcher remembers the early days of the estate.'We were the second occupants of Cepen Park South, moving into the house in August 1991. (It was built by) David Wilson homes. Apart from Sainsburys, there was just the block of show houses on Newbury Drive and our block of 5 houses (numbers 25-29) at the entrance of Ascot Close. The rest was a building site. The farmhouse was still there at that time.'

---

[310] Memories of Howard Clarke, Chippenham Street Names Facebook page.

12 - Allington & Cepen Park North

The name Allington comes from 'Atheling-ton'. *Atheling* is Anglo Saxon for 'prince' or 'noble heir', and *ton* for 'enclosure'.
Allington was originally a royal manor given by King Stephen to the nunnery of Martigny, which was in the upper valley of the Rhone. During the reign of Edward I it was transferred to the prior of Monkton Farleigh. At the dissolution of the monasteries, it was granted by Henry VIII to Sir Edward Seymour, the Duke of Somerset. By 1623, Allington had become the residence of Sir Gilbert Prynne of Bristol.
When Algernon, Duke of Somerset died in 1749 without an heir, Sir Charles Wyndham acquired the estate through titles. Eventually the estate was purchased by the Neeld family in 1844.[311]
The village of Allington is separated from the town by the A350 bypass road, which is currently in the process of a partial upgrade to a dual-carriageway.

The spectacular Prynne Memorial in St Andrew's church.

Allington Way is on the west side of Chippenham, in the direction of Allington village. It was the first part of the development, known as the 'Bristol Road Estate' during its construction. The estate has vehicular access from either Hungerdown Lane or Lords Mead.

Jill Hope was one of the first to live on the estate, and she recalls some of the early difficulties faced by families;

'The bungalows weren't built when we first moved in so we could play in the fields opposite. When the bungalows were built we were told not to play on the green as it would disturb the elderly residents.

---

[311] Wilts Arch and Nat Hist Soc.

This caused a bit of a dispute as the council had said it didn't matter about us having small back gardens, as there was all the open space for us to play in.'[312]

Phase one was built c1957, with houses fronting Hungerdown Lane, including some of those on Pipsmore Road, Barken Road and The Battens. **The Battens** is a reminder of Batten's Farm which belonged to William Baten in 1523.[313] Also, there is a memorial in St Andrew's church for Thomas Batten of Allington who died in 1628.[314]

Pipsmore Farm once covered part of this area, and gives its name to **Pipsmore Road.** This was recorded as 'Pippesmore' in 1270 and 'Popplesmore' in 1605.[315] A John Kipping rented 'Pipsmore Grounds' in 1683.

Barken Road - 'Barken' is a word which has long fallen out of common usage, which means 'made of bark'.

Phase two consisted of 140 homes built c1959 by Downing, Rudman and Bent on the southern section of the estate. This included the houses in Manor Road, additional on Pipsmore Road, Hither Close, Barn Close and part of the housing in Lamberts and Longstone Road. Also, some of the houses on part of Lords Mead, which at the time was called 'Isolation Hospital Lane'.[316]

Hither Close - 'Hither', in this context, comes from the old English *Hider*, which means a 'side or part of a hill or valley'.
Barn Close - Lord's Barn was nearby (see also Lords Mead).
Lamberts - The Lambert family kept land here. Henry Lambert was a mercer during the 17th century. He is recorded as a churchwarden in 1638 and bailiff of the borough in 1648.

---

[312] Jill Hope, Chippenham Street Names Facebook page.

[313] Gover, J.E.B., (1939), p.92

[314] Daniell, J.J., (1894), p.181.

[315] Gover, J.E.B., (1939), p.93

[316] G19/152/7, WSHC.

Manor Road - the manor of Allington. Many of the first residents of Manor Road were employees of MoD Copenacre and their families.[317]

Longstone Road is a reference to the 'long stone' on the road to Marshfield. This is the long barrow at Lanhill otherwise known as 'Hubba's Low' (see Lanhill View).

Off Bristol Road, just before Bumpers Farm Trading Estate, 'Fenway Park' was built c2006 by Redrow Homes. The tightly-knit network of streets make full use of available space. **Cornfields**, **Lower Field**, **Middle Leaze**, **Barley Leaze**, and **Middlefield Road** are all former field names. The streets were built on land previously occupied by Allington Boys School which closed in 1998.

Middlefield was also the name taken by the special school when it opened c1963. It stood on the corner of Hungerdown Lane and Bristol Road, but was recently demolished after being derelict since it closed in 2010. A supermarket and further housing is planned for the site.

Opposite Fenway Park, is the delightful **Mount Pleasant**. This was formerly a hamlet centred around a farm. The original 19th-century farmstead has unfortunately been demolished, but some period residential properties remain. These houses are the first reached on entering the town from the Bristol direction.

The Middlefield Centre after it closed. This has now been demolished and a supermarket is being built in its place. Photograph - Paul Budden-Schluefter.

An inscription on the terrace facing the main road reads; *'S. I. 1895 Mount Pleasant'*. This has been attributed to Samuel Isaac who had the terrace built for him by Downing & Rudman. The Isaac family lived at Bumpers Farm before the houses were built. The terrace was divided between three children of the Isaac family after Samuel died, each receiving two houses.[318]

Cepen Park North is made up of c800 homes located in the north-west of Chippenham. Between 1992 and 2003, the area was developed by a number of builders, led by Crest Nicholson.

---

[317] Jenny Robinson, Chippenham Street Names Facebook page.

[318] Keith House & Andy West, Chippenham Street Names Facebook page.

The older part of this estate used trees for the street names. **Willowbank, The Poplars, Jasmine Close, Mulberry Close, Hollybush Close, Blackberry Close, Acacia Close** are all found near the Bristol Road side of Cepen Park North.

Later additions followed with further inspiration from nature. The flower names; **Honeysuckle Close, Bluebell Drive, Buttercup Close, Celandine Way, Cowslip Way, Primrose Way, Selions Close, Sorrel Drive** are all found along the side of the estate which border the bypass road along with **Curlew Drive**, which begins a series of bird names used. These are; **Redwing Avenue, Robins Close, Sandpiper Gardens, Partridge Close, Barn Owl Road, Lapwing Crescent** and **Woodpecker Mews**.

Foxgrove, Fox Close, Sheepscroft and **Hares Patch** are also names inspired by nature on the estate.

Both **Argyle Drive** and **Sutherland Crescent** are close to Morrisons supermarket.

In November 1794 the 23rd Regiment of the Light Dragoons and the 98th Argyle and Sutherland regiment camped 'in and around' Chippenham, recruiting many men from the town during their stay.[319] In 1795, they moved to Spithead, and on 5th May embarked as part of Sir Alured Clarke's reinforcements for the British Army in South Africa. The 98th consisted of 738 men under the command of Lieutenant Colonel Duncan Campbell of Loch Nell. Out of the 32 officers, 17 were called Campbell![320]

Lanhill View faces the direction of Lanhill, two and a half miles from town, just past Allington on the A420. There is a Neolithic long barrow at Lanhill just off the main road, which was known as 'Hubba's Low'. Hubba, along with Guthrum, led the army of Danes who fought against King Alfred. He was slain in battle, and was believed to have been buried at this site. John Aubrey was the first to attribute this long barrow to Hubba, but it would have been built much earlier in around 3000 BC, than when the Danes were in the area.

Archaeologists have discovered approximately twenty burials inside, with ages ranging from a baby to older adults. The long barrow would have originally been 190 feet by 90 feet and 6 feet high. It is now in a sorry state due to modern farming and quarrying that took place indiscriminately over the site up until the 1960s. Some of the stones were even removed to repair the road close by.

---

[319] Bath Chronicle, 13 November 1794.

[320] Glasgow Herald, 21 March 1896.

In 1840, Lanhill was recorded as 'Lannell Hill' and may derive from 'Langenhill' meaning 'Long hill'.[321]

Barnes Road is named in honour of Alfred Barnes who was sexton of Hardenhush church for 39 years. He was responsible for church building maintenance and the upkeep of the graveyard. Barnes had also helped Captain Allfrey build the mansion at Greenways, and was later employed there as gardener. Greenways became the town maternity hospital on the formation of the NHS in 1948.
Barnes was a large part of life in the parish of Hardenhuish, and whilst sexton he 'served with loyalty and sincerity which won him the respect and esteem of the parishioners'. Further proof of his 'big missionary heart' was found after his death, when it was discovered that over the years, he had been giving all his church expense payments to charity.

Harnish Way - This is a local pronunciation and historical spelling of Hardenhuish.

Stainers Way - The Stainer family owned Upper Farm which was the land that much of Cepen Park North was built on. In the 1980s shortly before it was acquired for housing, it was an arable and beef producing farm with a herd of Friesian cows.

Other street names used for Cepen Park North are;
Fallow Field Close - a fallow field is one left to recover during the crop rotation system of farming.
Garth Close - a 'cloister garth' is a garden of a medieval monastery. There is also a detached property on Bath Road near the Ivy called 'The Garth'.
Chevral Close - Sir Alexander de Chevral owned Hardenhuish manor in the late 13th century. **Torr Close** - Torr Abbey was the home of the Cary family who owned a large part of Pewsham until 1791

---

[321] Gover, J.E.B., (1939), p.93.

13 - Frogwell and Derriads

Many of the streets in this area are named in honour of former town mayors.
The **Moss Mead** housing estate is to the north of Vincent's wood. Moss Mead itself, is named after Mrs Gertrude Emmeline Moss. In 1963 she became the town's second female mayor.
Noyes Close - The Noyes family gave two mayors to Chippenham. George Noyes was elected mayor in November 1865. He ran 'The Library' in the High Street, which was a book selling, printing and stationary business established in 1796. Mr JJ Fosters took over the business when George retired in 1872.[322]

'The Library' in the High Street, c1906.

George's son James followed in his fathers footsteps, becoming mayor for 1872 and 1873. Born in Chippenham where he remained all his life, James was an iron monger and the first mayor of the town to invest in ceremonial jewellery, purchasing a 'handsome chain and badge'.[323] He died in 1881 aged 61 at his home in Cook Street.

Townsend Place - Albert John Townsend had two terms as mayor in 1903 and 1915. Also, his son Albert George Townsend became mayor in 1932, when he succeeded his former headmaster Edward Newall Tuck.

Cruse Close - Herbert Arthur Cruse was an alderman, mayor and also general works manager of Westinghouse. Affectionately known as 'Bert', he lived at 'Andorinha', Hardenhuish with his wife Letitia and daughter Linda. Amongst his many public positions, he was governor of the Grammar School, vice chairman of the Chippenham Horticultural and Horse Society and president of the Chippenham Hospital League of Friends.

---

[322] Wiltshire Times, 1 October 1872.

[323] Wiltshire Times, 15 January 1881.

He received Queen Mary at Westinghouse during the Second World War when she visited to observe the manufacture of armaments there. During his time at the firm, he did much to improve the working conditions for the employees and received a CBE from the Queen at Buckingham Palace for 'public and industrial services'. These included acting as president of the Engineering and Allied Employers West of England Association and president of Chippenham Town Football Club. A keen sportsman, the purchase of land off Bristol Road for Westinghouse sports ground was possible largely because of his influence. He retired from his position as Works Manager at Westinghouse in 1954, having joined as an office boy in 1902. Cruse did much for the lives of many families in Chippenham, especially through his work at Westinghouse, and it is fitting that a street is named in his honour.[324] Cruse was mayor of Chippenham three times in 1951, 1952 and 1953.

Chamberlain Road - Joseph Archibald Chamberlain was appointed Principal of North West Wiltshire College of Further Education. He also was an author, writing a book on the history of Chippenham that was published in 1976. Chamberlain Road was built in the 1980s by Bradley's of Swindon and included the 3 bed detached 'Robinswood'.

The following streets were built in 1980 by EH Bradley & Sons, with their names chosen by the Charter Trustees after Bradleys waived their right to choose.[325]

Whittle Close - Mrs. Mona Sara Whittle was mayor in 1975 and was only the third woman in Chippenham's history to .
Phillips Close - Jacob Phillips of 'The Palace' served five times as mayor in 1842, 1852, 1857, 1861 and 1862. On his third departure as mayor a huge dinner party was held in the Angel Hotel with 120 guests including 'nearly all principal residents of the town'.
Jacob was a senior partner in Phillips and Creswick, Solicitors. He was 'called to the bar' in 1838. His other duties included being the Registrar of Chippenham County Court, Clerk to; the Board of Guardians, Assessment Committee, Rural Sanitary Committee and the Highway and burial boards.

---

[324] Wiltshire Times, 11 December 1954.

[325] G28/1/1/8/3, p.311, WSHC.

Jacob was also responsible for the erection of the clock on the tower of St Andrew's Church in 1858, which was paid for by public subscription.

Lastly, a worthy addition to the series of mayoral themed streets, **Awdry Close** recognises a whole family of mayors.
West Awdry was mayor in 1838. West lived at Monkton House in 1859.
He and his brother, Frederick Awdry were solicitors based in the Market Place. Frederick was mayor in 1848 and 1856.[326]
Another brother was Justly Awdry. He died in 1919 aged 100, and was one of Chippenham's oldest inhabitants at the time. He died at The Paddocks which was were he was born.
Justly was 'called to the bar' in 1843, practising as a solicitor in Melksham where he was also Officer in Command of the Melksham Company of Volunteers.

These medals were given to the school children of Chippenham to commemorate the coronation of King Edward VII in 1902. However, due to an outbreak of scarletina, this was delayed until January 1903.

He had the honours of being made Freeman of the Borough of Chippenham and was decorated by the King on his retirement.
On the 1939 register, Edmund Mainley Awdry is listed as a solicitor living at The Paddocks with his wife Rachel, daughter Janet and Son Michael. Michael Awdry is recorded as a public schoolmaster.
Edmund Mainley Awdry was mayor in 1885, 1886, 1896, 1901 and again in 1927. Both of his sons were also mayor; Edmund Portman Awdry in 1930, 1939, 1940, 1941 and 1942 and Neville John Awdry in 1945.
Edmund's son, Daniel Edmund Awdry, who was mayor in 1958 was also Conservative MP for Chippenham 1962 to 1979.

More mayoral themed streets can be found to the east of

---

[326] Post Office Directory, 1859.

Vincent's Wood;

Brinkworth Close - James Hancock Brinkworth was a coal merchant who began his business in 1828 using the canal from the wharf in Timber Street. He was a 'staunch liberal' politician, who was mayor in 1858 and served on the Board of Guardians helping those in poverty. Brinkworth was 'greatly respected' by the people of Chippenham. Miss Matilda Brinkworth, daughter of James, lived to be over 100 years old. She acted as mayoress during James' time as mayor, due to Mrs Brinkworth's untimely passing.[327]

Culverwell Road - George Lane Culverwell was mayor in 1936 and 1937. He was the son of Jasper Culverwell of Classey Farm, North Petherton, and came to Chippenham in 1914 to join the auctioneers Messrs Tilley and Parry, later becoming senior partner. During the First World War he served with the Wiltshire Yeomanry but was seconded to the Machine Gun Corps, in Eygpt and Palestine finishing as a Lieutenant whilst stationed in Beirut in 1919. George was the honorary secretary for both the Chippenham Chamber of Commerce and the Bath Christmas Market.

Mrs. Muriel Culverwell became the first female mayor of Chippenham in 1956. She held the unusual distinction of having served as mayoress for her husband, and then as mayor herself. She was the only daughter of Thomas Hosegood of Williton, Somerset. Mrs Culverwell came to Chippenham after she married Mr Culverwell in 1919. She was already prominent in public affairs before becoming a town and county councillor in 1947. Her work with the council centred on public health, housing, education and welfare. She also rallied the women of the town during the Second World War, organising a centre for the Women's Volunteer Services, for which she was awarded the British Empire Medal.
The Culverwell's regularly hosted events for religious or charitable organisations from their home at Lowden Manor, using the grounds in the summer for garden parties. Tennis tournaments were held to raise money for the hospital, and every year raised substantial funds.
Muriel took on the role of Carnival procession secretary and her husband George was chairman. Both had a long record of public service and were great contributors to the making of modern Chippenham.

---

[327] Wiltshire Times, 14 November 1936.

Ryan Avenue - A member of the Labour Party, Patrick L Ryan became mayor in 1946 after serving on the town council for sixteen years, succeeding Neville John Awdry.

Page Close - Henry William Page was mayor for 1966 and 1967.

South of Vincent's Wood, which maintained by Wiltshire Wildlife Trust since 1990, is the smaller, southern part of the wood which is an ancient woodland. Developers Bloor Homes built many of the properties here *c*1994.[328]

Turpin Way - Alfred Barrett Turpin, formerly of Oxford, was mayor in 1905 and a member of the Urban Sanitary Authority. He was also a chemist and druggist, coming to Chippenham from Oxford in 1883 to take over the business of Mr HF Draper, that formerly belonged to James Wharry. His shop in the High Street proudly advertised the sale of trusses, claiming to hold 'the largest stock in the south west of England.'[329]

Lenton Close - William George Lenton was mayor in 1934, succeeding Mr WE Vince who was the first Labour mayor of Chippenham, and had been successful in almost eliminating unemployment in the town. William was a keen fisherman, who put his skills of patience, used in his 'pursuit of piscatorial recreation', to good use as mayor. He was also vice chairman of the Borough Lands Committee.[330]

Collen Close - The Collen family were respected mill owners of the town mill at the bottom of Monkton Hill.[331]
Daniel Collen was a corn merchant, borough treasurer and a director of Chippenham Gas Company. He bequeathed money to various good causes when he died.[332] Daniel was mayor in 1889 and 1906 as a Liberal, whilst his brother George Walter Collen was a Conservative who was mayor in 1900.

---

[328] Alex Millard, Chippenham Street Names Facebook page.

[329] Wiltshire Times, 2 January 1892.

[330] Wiltshire Times, 17 November 1934.

[331] Platts, Arnold, (1947), p.74.

[332] Wiltshire Times, 31 March 1951.

Alice Maud Collen was the daughter of Daniel and lived at 'Lindenhurst' on Marshfield Road. Alice was a member of the choir of St Peter's church and a Sunday school teacher at St Paul's. With Lady Muriel Coventry she created the Chippenham and District Nursing Association, and on the Board of Guardians she had a keen interest in the 'boarding out' of children.

During the First World War she was largely responsible for the welfare, alongside Mr FJ Buden, of the Belgian refugees who were housed in the former West End Club after their evacuation from Belgium in 1914. The club was available due to the generosity of the Bath Brewery Company who had kindly allowed the use of their spacious premises for the refugees.[333]

Brittain Close - Frederick Charles Brittain succeeded Mr W Gee as mayor in 1944 at the age of 62, having already served on the town council for eleven years. Frederick was a former works manager at Westinghouse, making his way up the career ladder from a workman, and after his retirement was retained by the company in a 'consultative capacity.' A resident of Marshfield Road, he was a past Master of the Freemasons Lodge, a committee member for the secondary school evening classes and the Vice President of the local British Legion branch. He served his country in India with the Wiltshire Territorials and received a battlefield commission with the 2nd Battalion Wiltshire Regiment in France during the First World War.

Barons Mead is part of the 'Lords Mead Estate' built in 1962 by AJ Wait & Co. Initially, the council approved the developers' suggestion of calling this street 'Lords Mead Crescent'. The Head Postmaster did not agree that this name was suitable, as there was already a Lords Mead, and any 'illegibly addressed' letters would cause confusion. The council recommended the name 'Barons Mead' instead.[334]

A 'Baron's Charity' is recorded as receiving a contribution of nine shillings from Bumpers Farm in 1888, and it is likely that this was an inspiration for the council's choice.[335] This charity may have links to John Baron, who was one of the trustees named on the original Maud Heath Trust document in 1474.

---

[333] Western Daily Press, 28 October 1914.

[334] G19/100/19, p.340 & p.380, WSHC.

[335] G19/100/4, p.16, WSHC.

The following streets have roughly been given a royal theme;
Balmoral Close - Balmoral Castle is a royal residence built between 1852 and 1856 by William Smith. The Balmoral castle bridge was built by Brunel using ironwork made in Chippenham at Rowland Brotherhood's foundry. **Weavers Close** is off Balmoral Close. These two streets were built c1997.
Fredericks Avenue may be named after somebody with this surname, but as yet it has not been possible to explain this.
Clarence Road - Clarence House is a royal residence built by John Nash between 1825 and 1827. It was the home of HRH the Queen Mother from 1953 to 2002, and now that of the Prince of Wales and the Duchess of Cornwall.
Kensington Way - Kensington Palace was built by Sir George Coppin in 1605.
Kings Avenue - Royal theme continued. Kensington Way and Kings Avenue were both built c1995 by Beazer Homes, Alfred McAlpine and Bloor Homes.

The name Derriads comes from the old english word *deor*, which translates as 'animal', and *geard*, which is a 'yard' or 'enclosure'. In other words, it is a place where animals are kept. Derriads was recorded as 'Derrits' in 1773.
The **Derriads Green** development was built here after the end of the Second World War in 1946, and was for war workers who had been put up in temporary housing at nearby Frogwell.[336]
As the housing in this area increased, **Derriads Lane** was declared a new street in 1961. Towards the end of the lane, is **Derriads House**, which was the home of the Goldney family. The house is a Grade II listed 17th-century property built in Bath Stone. After the Second World War it became a children's home and in the early 1980s it was converted into five separate residences.

Derriads Green Coronation party in 1953. Photograph - Eddie Kearton.

At the far end of Derriads Lane is **Derriads Court**. This was built next to Derriads Farm which is first recorded in 1167. An avenue of trees ran from Hungerdown Lane to Derriads, and many of these are still to be found in the gardens of Truro Walk, Coniston Road and Queens Crescent.

---

[336] Platts, Arnold, (1947), p.69.

When **Down View** was built there would have been nothing to block the view of the countryside before it. Positioned on the edge of Hungerdown, which may also have provided inspiration for the name.

Gascelyn Close is named after the Gascelyn family.
The Town coat of arms Is made up of the arms of two families; the Gascelyn family of Sheldon, and the Husee family of Rowden. The Gascelyns were the owners of the manor of Sheldon from 1250 to 1424. During this time they were granted permission from the Crown, for two three-day fairs on 17 May and 22 June each year. The shield of Sir Walter Gascelyn; 'a golden field surmounted by ten billets azure and a label gules', forms the *dexter* side of the Borough arms. The manor of Sheldon was incorporated into the borough in 1856.[337]
The *sinister* side of the borough arms has 'three boots sable', which is the symbol of the Husse family of the manor of Rowden.
In between the two shields is a palm tree, which is not believed to have any special significance and is purely decorative. The motto was added much later.[338]

Drake Crescent, **Heron Way** and **Pheasant Close** are all named after birds, probably to reflect the type of wildlife found close by. Developers tend to choose such names, hoping to attract buyers, using a countryside theme. **Oak Road**, **Hazel Copse** and **Meadow Close** are further examples nearby.

Frogwell is a name which has been in use for hundreds of years. An early spelling of Frogwell, 'Froggehull', was recorded in 1274.[339]

---

[337] Platts, Arnold, (1947), p.5.

[338] White, George A.H., (1924), p.4.

[339] Gover, J.E.B., (1939), p.93.

Lords Mead is named after Lords Barn. This barn was used by the Lord family in the 17th century. Thomas Lord is recorded here in 1642.[340]

The new St Peter's church was built in Lords Mead and was consecrated on 7 December 1968. It is a six sided structure built using brick and reconstituted stone, topped off with a copper roof and a fibreglass spire. There are no internal supports to ensure a clear view for the whole congregation. St Peter's Primary School was built next to the church and opened in October 1973.

During the first half of the last century, Lords Mead was known as 'Isolation Hospital Lane', and is marked as such on a 1959 plan of the 'Allington Housing Estate'. An isolation hospital equipped with 32 beds was built here in 1899 at a cost of £1,372. Later it became Frogwell Hospital. This shut in the 1980s and was sold for housing, becoming **Frogwell Park**. Before this facility was built, there was an 'Isolation hut' erected in 1896 at Hulberts Hold, near Rowden Farm.

Picketleaze is probably an old field name, as a 'leaze' is a meadow. Building began here in 1973 by EH Bradley & Sons of Swindon.[341] The first residents moved in from 1975.[342]

Frogwell School Football Team c1973. Photograph - Mike Bowden.

Westbrook Close is west off Ladyfield Brook and was built by Smith & Lacy in 1964.[343]

Frogwell Primary School is opposite the appropriately named **School Walk**. The school was opened in 1943, initially on a temporary basis for evacuees and the children of transferred war workers.[344] As the town expanded to the west, more primary schools were required.

Beale Court is close to Frogwell School, and is named after Joan Stopford Beale, who was well known and respected in Chippenham.

---

[340] Gover, J.E.B., (1939), p.92.

[341] G19/100/25, p.463, WSHC.

[342] Memories of Marcia Bull, Chippenham Street Names Facebook page.

[343] G19/100/23, p.301, WSHC.

[344] Platts, Arnold, (1947), p.54.

She was a teacher during the early days of Frogwell School, and sat on the Borough Education Board and Planning Committee.[345] She was also chair of the Chippenham Grammar School Old Pupils Association, and the chair of Governers of Sheldon School when it opened in 1959.[346] She was present at the naming ceremony of Beale Court, named after her in recognition of her services to local education.[347]

Weavern Court accompanies Beale Court. The definition of 'Weavern' is wavering, and the River Bybrook which runs to the west of Chippenham used to be known as 'The Weavern'. Both Beale Court and Weavern Court were built c1985.

---

[345] Memories of Trisha Lewis, Chippenham Street Names Facebook page.

[346] Wiltshire Times, 16 January 1954.

[347] Memories of Andy Stovell, Chippenham Street Names Facebook page.

14 - Pewsham

The name Pewsham comes from a small stream called 'Pewe Brook', which begins at Pitter's Farm in Studley, passes under the canal by means of a culvert at Pewsham Locks, and joins the Bristol Avon near Lackham college two and a half miles later. The modern name of the Pewe is Cocklemere Brook. The village of Pewsham is not actually a part of Chippenham or its parish, and as such it had no ecclesiastical existence such as a church, yet was liable to pay tithes.[348] Early variations of the spelling of Pewsham include; 'Pevisham' in 1448 and 'Pevesham' in 1449.[349]
The area concerned by this book is the Pewsham housing estate, which is part of the modern town.

Many of the streets in Pewsham reflect the history of the former canal. **Canal Road** is the most obvious example, but some are less so, such as **Windlass Way**. A windlass is the name of the handle used to open the lock gates on a canal. **Waters Edge**, **Lockside**, **Pewsham Lock**, refer to the proximity of the route of the canal, to the housing development.
Plans were first put forward for the construction of a Chippenham arm of the Wiltshire and Berkshire canal on 8 February 1792.[350] Special permission was required to enable the route to pass through Borough lands at Inglands (Englands) in 1794.[351] The canal originally ended here, and in 1801 sheds were built for the use by the barge masters and other tradesman connected to the building and repair of barges.[352] By 1798 the canal had reached Englands and from 1800 was extended to a coal wharf in Timber Street, after passing through a tunnel which still partially exists under Wood Lane and Burlands Road today.

---

[348] Daniell, J.J., (1894), pp.56.

[349] Gover, J.E.B., (1939), p.108.

[350] Platts, Arnold, (1947), p.82.

[351] Goldney, F. H., (1889), p.104.

[352] Goldney, F. H., (1889), p.113.

Whitworth Road - Robert Whitworth and his son William surveyed and engineered the canal construction which took place between 1795 and 1810.

The main cargo transported on the canal was Somerset Coal, but others such as building materials and agricultural produce were also moved in this way. There was a decline in its use from the second half of the 19th century and the canal eventually closed in 1904. The main reason was that the railways became the more popular choice. The disused canal was used as a tip for many years afterwards.

Many of the streets in Pewsham are named after notable individuals who either lived, owned land in, or represented the town in some way.

Hawkins Close - Thomas Hawkins was a leading clothier in Chippenham during the 17th century. Also one of the burgesses of the borough, he died in 1676 and his memorial is in St Andrew's Church.[353]
In 1689, a Mrs Hawkins left the interest on £10 to be paid by the Bailiff to six poor widows of freemen of the borough.[354] This was paid at Candlemas (February 2nd) each year by the bailiff of the borough.

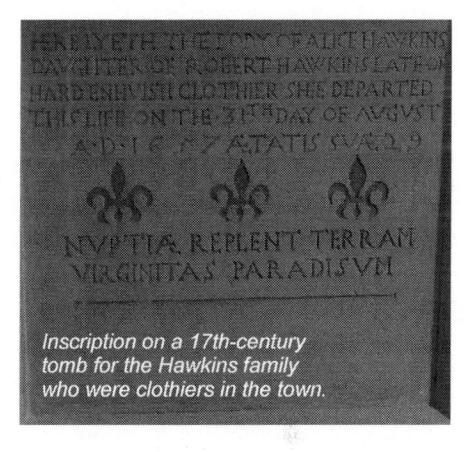

Inscription on a 17th-century tomb for the Hawkins family who were clothiers in the town.

Daniell Drive - John Jeremiah Daniell, 1819 to 1898, was the rector of Langley Burrell parish church. Historian and antiquarian, he was the author of *The History of Chippenham* in 1894. Daniell's other works included *The History of Warminster* in 1879, where he was previously curate.

Brotherton Close - The reasons behind the naming of this street remain uncertain. A Robert Brotherton, Congregational Minister resided in the town in 1939 and in more recent times the URC in Emery Lane was officiated by the Rev Georgina Brotherton. Either of these may be the inspiration behind the name, but further enquiries will need to be made.

---

[353] Daniell, J.J., (1894), p.167.

[354] Daniell, J.J., (1894), p.163.

Lysley Close would make most people think of the Lysley Arms public houses at the bottom of Derry Hill, formerly the Swan Inn. The Lysleys were a prominent local family. William John Lysley was Liberal MP for Chippenham and lived in Pewsham. The July 1865 riots were due to the election defeat of Lysley.[355] Despite a large public support, he was unsuccessful in his campaign that year, and Sir John Neeld and Sir Gabriel Goldney were returned. A mob of around 500 men, women and children assembled in the Market Place, overpowered the small police force and destroyed the property of the Conservatives in the town. Goldney was chased across the Market Place to the churchyard, where tombstones were torn out and thrown through the Conservatives office and vicarage windows. The Times described Chippenham on that day as the 'palm of barbarism and brutality'.[356]

Maitland Close - In 1801, John Maitland was put forward to be an MP for Chippenham but lost to Charles Brooke. He petitioned against the vote and successfully obtained the seat. In 1806 he was re elected along with Charles Brooke. A full account of the 1801 dispute can be found in *Peckwell's collection of controverted elections.*[357]
Also, Ebenezer Fuller Maitland was MP for Chippenham in 1826.

Other streets named after former Chippenham MP's include; **Thomas Mead** after Sir Edward Thomas MP and **Ailesbury Close** after the 5th Marquess of Ailesbury MP.

Anglesey Mead and **Christopher Drive** after both named after one individual, Christopher Villiers the 1st Earl of Anglesey. Villiers was granted lands, which included Pewsham forest, in 1624. His 'disafforesting of Pewsam' in 1630, caused a riot, and the Countess of Anglesey was held captive by rebels. George Cary a later heir to the Earldom of Anglesey sold the forest, which divided it up between the Lysley and Bruges families as well as the Montagus of Lackham.

---

[355] Platts, Arnold, (1947), pp.45-46.

[356] Daniell, J.J., (1894), p.111.

[357] Goldney, F. H., (1889), pp.117-121.

Castlehaven Close - John Tuchet, the 5th Earl of Castlehaven, was married to Anne Pelson. Anne was was the daughter of Christopher Villiers.

Buckingham Road George Villiers was Christopher's brother. He was the 1st Duke of Buckingham and favourite of King James I. These streets were part of the 'Petersfield Park' development built by Edwin Bradley of Swindon, c1981. Bradley's were best known for being employed in the reconstruction of Avebury Neolithic stone circle in 1939.

Pembroke Road - The Earl of Pembroke was High Steward of Chippenham in 1568.[358]

Danvers Mead - The Danvers were a Puritan family from Dauntsey. Sir John Danvers had a daughter who was Walter Hungerford's second wife.

Sherrington Mead - Sir William Sherrington of Lacock owned the Manor of Sheldon after Lord Hungerford.[359] The homes here were built c1984 by Wimpey.

Ray close is named after Ray's charity of 1615. Thomas Ray left his house and thirteen small tenements in Sarum (Salisbury) for the benefit of the 'poor clothiers' of Chippenham, Westbury, Trowbridge and Marlborough, each taking a turn to benefit.[360]

Provis Mead - From 1812, local character John Provis and his family lived at Orwell House, which was later the home of the Brotherhood family. Provis was a timber merchant and builder and was involved in contracts linked to the Great Western Railway. His timber yard was opposite Orwell House. He was a general all-rounder and public spirited, giving lectures on the history of Chippenham and investing much of his time working for the benefit of others. For example, he tried to invent improvements in shipping techniques to reduce the loss of life through shipwrecks. He also

---

[358] Daniell, J.J., (1894), p.66.

[359] Daniell, J.J., (1894), p.14.

[360] Daniell, J.J., (1894), p.163.

had a large library of books and a collection of fossils which were all found in North Wiltshire.[361] [362]

His son Alfred showed advance intellect at a young age, so John built him a studio in their garden and arranged for him to have tuition in painting with oils. Later Alfred studied under John Wood in London and his works soon gained recognition, and displayed in exhibitions such as at the Royal Academy of Art. His work included local scenes, such as *Chippenham Market Place*. Alfred died in 1890 aged 72, leaving an unfinished collection, including a sketch entitled *Shambles, Chippenham*. One of his paintings was recently acquired by Chippenham Museum.

In 1621 the bells were rung as James I passed through the town.[363] It is more likely, however, that **James Close** is named after James II, who restored the Charter originally granted by Queen Mary, when he also passed through the town in 1687.[364]

Holland Close - Rogers Holland was MP for Chippenham from 1727 to 1737.
The 'Chippenham Spa' was situated in the garden of Judge Holland in St Mary Street, which added to the town's reputation of being known as 'Little Bath'.

Hewlett Close - James Hewlett (1768 to 1836) was the son of a gardener of Monkton. Despite his lowly background, he learnt to paint to a exceptional standard, and even had is work exhibited at the Royal Academy.[365] Hewlett was a contemporary and good friend of John Britton.
When Hewlett Close was built in 1986, a three-bed corner terrace property costing £26,125.[366]

Anstey Place - Christopher Anstey is described as a 'lively but not voluminous poet', who was educated at Kings College in Cambridge. He was destined for a career in the Church, but

---

[361] Baines, Richard, (2009), p.128

[362] Wiltshire Times, 1 September 1923.

[363] Daniell, J.J., (1894), *The History of Chippenham*.

[364] Daniell, J.J., (1894), pp.62.

[365] Daniell, J.J., (1894), p.212.

[366] Gabrielle Garland, Chippenham Street Names Facebook page.

unexpectedly inherited a moderate fortune which enabled him to pass his time leisurely at Bath. His most significant work was *The New Bath Guide*, which was described as a 'new and diverting species of poetry', and was sufficient to earn him a heritage plaque at 5 Royal Crescent, Bath and a commemoration at Poet's Corner in Westminster Abbey. Anstey died at Hardenhuish in 1805, aged 81.[367]

Colborne Close - The Colborne family played a significant part in the history of Chippenham. It was Joseph Colborne who commissioned John Wood the Younger to design Hardenhuish Church.
William Henry Colborne was a physician who practised in St Mary Street. He was also mayor of Chippenham in 1846, 1850 and 1851.

Bradbury Close - Notable Bradbury inhabitants of Chippenham include;
Edward Bradbury died in 1897 aged 82. For 64 years he was an employee of Messrs Awdry & Awdry, and was assistant to Mr West Awdry when he was clerk to the Board of Guardians. He was also connected to Chippenham Savings Bank. However, he was perhaps best known as being the Registrar of Chippenham for 52 years, responsible for recording births, marriages and deaths. He possessed a 'wonderful memory' and was held in great esteem by his large circle of friends. He lived at the Folly on Bristol Road, but ended his days at Prospect Lodge in Corsham. Bradbury was also also a member of the Plymouth Brethren.[368]

There is a memorial to William and Clementina Bradbury in St Andrew's, who died 1763 and 1785 respectively.[369]

This street however, like others nearby, is named after a Bradbury whose charitable actions have benefitted the town in some way. In 1834, Ann Bradbury left the interest on £100 to be used for blankets for the poor, on the condition that every fifth year the money would be put towards the restoration of her sisters tomb.[370]

---

[367] A new Biographical dictionary, Stephen Jones.

[368] Wiltshire Times, 9 October 1897.

[369] Daniell, J.J., (1894), p.175.

[370] Daniell, J.J., (1894), p.164.

Gundry Close is named after William Gundry who was the mayor of Chippenham in 1837. There is a memorial to William and his wife Ruth, who died in 1853 and 1855 in St Andrew's, but they are actually buried in Backwell Church in Somerset.[371] In William's will dated 1851, he left £500 in trust to the Vicar and his Wife.

Elizabeth Place must surely be named after Elizabeth I, who is arguably our greatest monarch.

Rooks Nest Close - Rooks Nest Farm was an 18th-century farmstead of which the sole survivor is the farmhouse, which **Farmhouse Close** is named after.
A 'close called Rook Nest' was occupied by John Heath in 1788.[372]
Ludlow Close is named after the Ludlow family. William Henry Ludlow Bruges was MP of Chippenham and Chairman of the Chippenham Union. Rooks Nest Farm belonged to Mrs Ludlow Bruges in 1864.[373]
Notably, Stephen Edward Hart was a dairy farmer here for over sixty years upon retiring, according to his obituary in 1937.[374]
Rooks Nest Farmhouse stands in **Forest Lane**, which is named after Pewsham Forest, a great forest belonging to the Crown, hence **Crown Close**. The Domesday book of 1086 records the forest as six miles square.[375]
Homes were built here between 1987 and 1991 by Walter Lawrence Homes.
Cary Glen Edward Cary of Torr Abbey in Devon, passed on his ownership of a large part of Pewsham to his son George Cary. George sold this in 1791 to the Montague family of Lackham.

The remains of Stanley Abbey, from which Abbeyfield Secondary school takes its name, can still be found in a garden just off the disused railway line at Stanley. The origins of this Abbey are remembered by **Lockswell Close**, which takes its name from Lockswell Spring. A group of Cistercian monks settled at Lockswell, which was in the south of Pewsham forest, and in 1151 began to build an abbey close to the famous springs. Lockswell Abbey farm

---

[371] Daniell, J.J., (1894), p.180.

[372] Goldney, F.H., (1889), p.101.

[373] Wiltshire Times, 21 October 1864.

[374] Wiltshire Times, 24 April 1937.

[375] Platts, Arnold, (1947), p.6.

house is believed to be the remnants of the former monastic buildings and reservoir. Three years later due to an additional grant of meadow land, they moved to Stanley. There they used the river to form fish ponds and power a mill. The mill was still working, and an abutment from the original bridge was still in existence, as late as the early 19th century. In 1214, the monks built an underground conduit for the Lockswell Spring in order to carry it to their new home three miles away. It would have been made of stone and 'large enough to admit a boy'. Edward I granted a licence to the Abbott to dry iron in the forest. The abbey was sold by Henry VIII after the dissolution, to Sir Edward Baynton in 1537 for £1,200. This in turn descended to the Starkeys of Spye Park and later the land became part of that which belonged to the Marquis of Lansdowne of Bowood.[376]

King John, Edward I and Edward II are all recorded to have stayed at Stanley Abbey, where there were thirteen white monks and many lay brothers, with a total population possibly close to 100 people.[377] During the construction of the 'Calne Bunk' branch line 1863, which passed through lands that had previously belonged to the Abbey, a group of about a dozen burials were discovered. Interestingly the skeletons were positioned in the prone position (face down), a method when deliberate, usually reserved as a mark of disrespect towards the deceased. Also, at a level of seven feet below the surface, was unearthed a blacksmiths forge, with fresh coal.[378]

The fate of the abbey, like so many others throughout the country, was sealed by Henry VIII and his dissolution of the monasteries. **Monks Way**, **Abbey Close**, along with **Tudor Close** and **King Henry Drive** are reminders of when 'hideous Henry smote to the dust' Stanley Abbey in 1536.[379]

Scorched grass reveals the canal in Tudor Close. Photograph - Caroline Fowke.

---

[376] Daniell, J.J., (1894), pp.48-54.

[377] Daniell, J.J., (1894), p.53.

[378] Daniell, J.J., (1894), p.54.

[379] Platts, Arnold, (1947), p.9.

Encaustic tiles and sculptured stones were salvaged from the ruins and assembled in an oratory at Bremhill vicarage garden by William Bowles the poet.[380]

Fitzwarren Close is named after Fluke Fitzwarren, who had his lands confiscated by King John in the 12th century. The legend tells that Fluke Fitzwarren, whilst playing with Prince John when they were boys, checkmated him in a game of chess. John hit Fluke on the head with the board and Fluke in turn knocked him down. John went crying to his father, Henry II, but he had no sympathy and beat him for losing. John never forgot, and when he became King he took all of Fluke's estates.
Fluke's followers including Barons who opposed John's tyranny, pursued a private war against the King. Fluke and his band of men hid in Pewsham Forest, in a manner reminiscent of the tale of Robin Hood. He was hunted by the Crown and in 1202 hid in Stanley Abbey where he was besieged for fourteen days.[381]

Blackthorn Mews, **Bramble Drive** and **Hedge Row** are all names that reflect the close countryside that Pewsham borders.

Webbington Road. Webbington is believed to mean 'the weaving enclosure', from the Old English *webbian* and *tun*.

The Pewsham estate has been partly built on former Borough lands which were gifted to the town at its incorporation by Queen Mary (see Charter Road). Streets which are named after these fields are; **Blackwellhams** which was a meadow, **Bolts Croft** which was grazing land, **Claypole Mead** a meadow known as 'Claypoles', and **Humbolts Hold**.

Danes Close - The Danes were besieged by Alfred the Great at Chippenham, after they had previously driven Alfred out and to Somerset.
Lodge Road - King Alfred's Hunting Lodge was believed to be just off what is now the Market Place in the town centre. Pewsham was originally forest and fenced off to keep in the Royal Deer for the sport of the nobility, *c*1299.
The shops and main centre of facilities for Pewsham are off Lodge Road. As is often the case, these were built after much of the housing was finished, with a portakabin acting as a doctors surgery

---

[380] Daniell, J.J., (1894), p.53.

[381] Daniell, J.J., (1894), p.51.

and community hub as late as 1988.[382] When completed they were officially opened by television actor Bill Roach, best known for his role as Ken Barlow in *Coronation Street*.[383] It seems that celebrity openings were popular with developers. Cheryl Baker of the 1980s pop group *Bucks Fizz*, cut the ribbon on one phase of homes here in 1995.

It is unknown whether Chippenham was inhabited during the Roman period but there are Roman sites and roads in the vicinity, and Roman artefacts have been found in the town. A group of streets in Pewsham are a reminder of this connection; **Centurion Close**, **Roman Way**, **Legate Close**. A Centurion was an officer in the Roman army in command of one hundred soldiers. Legate is the anglicised version of 'Legatus' meaning Roman General. Recently an impressive piece of Roman Samian Ware was unearthed in the garden of BBC Antiques Roadshow expert Marc Allum in St Mary Street. The dig was part a project called 'Seeking Saxon Chippenham', which has undertaken a number of excavations in the garden which was the original St Andrews Rectory. The pottery has the image of a lion and a gladiator on it, and will be restored for public display in 2019.

Norman Close some of the earliest records of Chippenham exist as a result of the Norman Conquest. The Domesday book of 1086 was a survey commissioned by William the Conqueror to assess the value of property, land and livestock covering all settlements in the country. It records Chippenham as 'Cepen'.

A large number of streets on the Pewsham Estate are named after the fallen of the two world wars. The former curator of Chippenham Museum was

Chippenham War Memorial stands in the Market Place on the site of the old town water pump. Many of the names on here have been used as street names in Pewsham. Postcard sent in 1931.

---

[382] Jackie Molesworth, Chippenham Street Names Facebook page.

[383] Gabrielle Garland et al, Chippenham Street Names page.

asked by the council to come up with a list of names, so chose ones listed on the Town Memorial in the Market Place. This next section of the chapter is more of a list, which is deliberate as it is itself like a memorial within the book. This change of pace will hopefully emphasise to the reader how much the town was affected by war in the 20th century. It must be remembered that these names are not all of those from the town who died in the two world wars, as unfortunately there were many more.

The information on these men, has come from various sources including the Commonwealth War Graves Commission, local newspapers and the excellent *pro-patria.co.uk*.

Bishops Close - Pioneer Albert George Bishop of the 87th Field Company Royal Engineers, died of his wounds whilst serving in France aged 21 on 20 July 1915. Albert is remembered on the Causeway Methodist memorial as HAH Bishop. Born and raised in nearby North Wraxall, he was the son of George and Jane Bishop and is also listed on the North Wraxall village memorial.

Knights Close - George Alfred Knight was born in London but was a resident of Chippenham before joining up. A Private in the 1/4th Wiltshire Regiment, he was killed in action in Jerusalem on 22 November 1917.

The Avon Meadows development by Heron Homes was built in 1988 off Canal Road. It consisted of 64 detached Four-Bedroomed homes on; Fox Croft Walk, Millard Close, Chandler Way, Granger Close, Milford Way and Bodman Close. All six of these streets are named after soldiers who died whilst serving with the Wiltshire Regiment during the First World War.

Bodman Close - George Bodman was a Private in the 5th Wiltshire Regiment and was the son of John and Annie Bodman of 'Avondale Villa' 1 London Road. George died of wounds aged 19 in Mesopotamia (Iraq) on 12 January 1917. He had previously served at Gallipoli, and was underage when he first enlisted.

Chandler Way - Clive Chandler was a Second Lieutenant in the 1st Battalion Wiltshire Regiment. One of the 'Old Contemptibles', Clive died early in the war on 17 November 1914 at Ypres.

Fox Croft Walk - Joseph Stanley Victor Fox was born in Corsham and lived at 45 Causeway. He was a Lance Corporal in 1st Battalion Wiltshire Regiment, but was attached to 3rd Division Cyclist Company, when he deserted. Aged only 20, he was caught, tried

and then executed on 20 April 1915 at Dickebusch, Ypres. His parents, Charles and Harriet Fox, also of 45 Causeway, did not receive confirmation of their sons death from the War Office, but rather by word from a fellow soldier who knew Joseph. It seems that the manner of his death was not shared and Charles Fox soon joined up to fight 'The Hun' and avenge his son's death.
After the war, Joseph was added to the Town Memorial, which would not have been allowed if it was known that he was 'shot at dawn'. It has been assumed, that due to an error, whether deliberate or otherwise, nobody found out about Joseph's cause of death and he was commemorated, as he should have been, as another brave victim of war.[384]

Granger Close - William Thomas Granger lived at 40 Park Lane. William served with the 4th Wiltshire Regiment in India, then was later commissioned as a Lieutenant and attached to the 6th Wilts on the Western Front. He died of wounds on the Menin Road in Belgium on 21 September 1917. He was aged 24. A former assistant Scout Master in the town, William had later worked in Swindon for GWR as a railway porter. He was a former member of the choir of St Paul's church and is commemorated on the memorial there as well as on the main memorial in the Market Place.

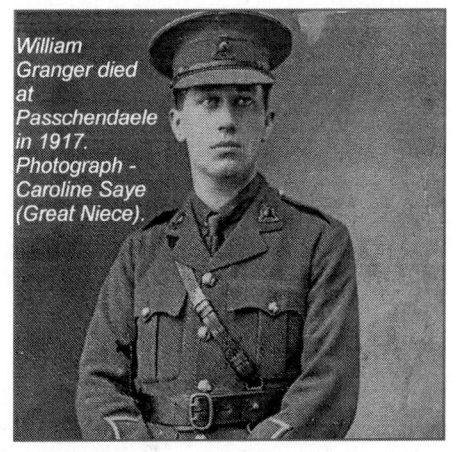

William Granger died at Passchendaele in 1917. Photograph - Caroline Saye (Great Niece).

Milford Way - James William Milford lived at 16 Wood Lane with his wife Rose, and was the son of Charles William Milford. On 28 November 1915 aged 30, he died of exposure during a heavy blizzard, whilst serving as a Private in 5th Battalion Wiltshire Regiment at Gallipoli.

Millard Close - Albert Edward Millard was a Private in the 2nd Battalion Wiltshire Regiment. Born in Stanton St Quentin, Albert was the son of Charles and Emily Millard. Sadly, Albert was killed on the Somme aged 25 on 8 August 1916.

---

[384] http://www.pro-patria.co.uk

Private George Millard was also serving with the 2nd Battalion Wiltshire Regiment, when he died of wounds received in France on 24 March 1918 aged 29. George was the son of Mrs EB Jones of 31 Timber Street.

The next group of streets off Canal Road were built by Walter Lawrence Homes c1988.

Beaven Close - Frank Beaven was the son of William and Rebecca Beaven of 3 Victoria Buildings, 46 London Road. Frank was a Royal Navy Able Seaman serving on the HMS Queen Mary during the Battle of Jutland when he died aged 23 on 31 May 1916.

Brewer Mead - Private William Arthur Brewer of the 1st Battalion Wiltshire Regiment, was only 21 when he was declared 'missing presumed dead' at Ypres on 13 November 1914. William was the son of George and Sarah Brewer of 81 Wood Lane. He was a footballer having success with Chippenham Town and making appearances for Swindon Town Reserves. As well as being commemorated on the Menin Gate memorial, William is listed on the Liberal Club, Causeway Methodist, Congregational and Swindon Town FC memorials.

Brewer Mead also remembers Private Charles Brewer of the 7th Somerset Light Infantry who died whilst serving in Normandy on 9 August 1944.

Escott Close - Frederick Escott was a Private in the 2nd Wiltshire Regiment when he was killed at Neuve Chapelle on March 11 1915. Before the war he worked for the Great Western Railway signal section. He was the youngest son of William and Annie Escott of 102 Wood Lane.

Holmes Close - Kenneth James Holmes, was a native of Hull. He married Mary Vaughan of the George Hotel, High Street. He joined the RAF as an aircraft apprentice at the age of 16, and had rose to the rank of Pilot Officer for 217 Squadron Coastal Command, by the age of 26. In 1941 he was awarded the Distinguished Flying Cross for his courage whilst attacking the German battle cruisers 'Scharnhorst' and 'Gneisenau' which were harboured in Brest, whilst under heavy anti aircraft fire. Unfortunately he never made his investiture at Buckingham Palace, as he died six weeks later on 18 June 1941, as the result of an accident near Devizes at RAF Alton Barnes involving a collision with another allied aircraft.

Sheppard Close - Reginald Edward Sheppard was a Private in the 1st/4th Battalion Northumberland Fusiliers. He was born in Chippenham and lived with his Father, Samuel Sheppard, at 1 Springfield Buildings. Reginald died in France on 14 February 1918 aged 25 and was buried at Bucquayid Cemetery in Ficheux.

Stewart Close - Dennis Maurice Stewart served as a Flying Officer in 280 Squadron of the RAF Volunteer Reserves. He was flying in a Vickers Warwick aircraft carrying out Air Sea Rescue duties on 13 November 1943, when his plane crashed. Dennis died aged 29 and was buried at Stonefall cemetery in Harrogate, Yorkshire. His wife Olive Mercia Stewart lived at Branksome Park, Bournemouth.

Swanborough Close - Arthur Henry John Swanborough of Wood Lane was a Private in the 1st Gloucestershire Regiment. He was shot in the lungs at Mons and died of his wounds at Chippenham Cottage Hospital on the 10 April 1915 aged only 20. As he was discharged from the Army before his death, he was not entitled to a military funeral and was buried in an unmarked grave at London Road cemetery. John Belcher, the creator of *pro-patria.co.uk*, was instrumental in the campaign to have his burial site properly recognised. The Commonwealth War Graves Commission has since marked the spot with one of their gravestones.

Private Arthur Swanborough who was buried in an unmarked grave, now has a fitting memorial for his family to visit.

William Arthur Swanborough was born in Chippenham but lived at 17 Sladebrook, Bradford on Avon with his wife Hilda Nellie Swanborough. His parents Joseph and Fanny Swanborough were living at 5 Lowden Avenue when their son was killed in action in Israel on 7 November 1917. William was serving with the 1st/4th Battalion Wiltshire Regiment when he died, and is buried at the Gaza war cemetery.

Willis Close - Frederick Willis was born in Bremhill near Calne but was a resident of Chippenham. He served with the 2nd Battalion Wiltshire Regiment as a Private and was declared missing presumed dead on 9 April 1917. Frederick is commemorated on the Arras memorial.

Another group off Canal Road

Bright Close - George Frederick Bright was a Private in the 6th Battalion Wiltshire Regiment. He was born in Bath, but was living in Chippenham when he enlisted at the age of 19. He died aged 21 on 3 November 1916 on the Somme and is commemorated on the Theipval memorial. George was the son of Thomas and Kate Bright of 20 Emery Lane.

Albert Edward Bright was a Corporal in the 17th/21st Lancers when he died aged 28 on 21 February 1943 at Kasserine in Tunisia. He is commemorated on the Medjez-el-bab memorial.

Frank Augustus Bright was a Sergeant in 'A' Squadron of the 12th Royal Lancers. He died in Italy on 4 January 1945. Frank was the son of Walter Inkerman Bright and Sarah Ellen Bright and the husband of Freda Maud Bright of Calne.

Carpenter Close - Thomas Henry Carpenter of 10 London Road, was the husband of Lydia Jane Carpenter. Thomas served on the Western Front as a Private in the 2nd Battalion Leinster Regiment, previously with the Dorsetshire Regiment. He was killed in action on the Somme on 27 March 1918.

Fortune Way - Herbert Thomas James Fortune was a Private in the 2nd Battalion of the Devonshire Regiment. He was born in Calne but later lived with his parents Thomas and Mary Jane Fortune at 'Fair view' 1 Sheldon Road. He was killed in action at Aisne in France on 31 March 1918. Herbert is also commemorated on the Causeway Methodist memorial.

Harford Close - Staff Sergeant Richard Jesse Harford of the Royal Army Ordnance Corps died aged 29 on 19 September 1942 whilst serving in India. Richard was the husband of Florence Vera Harford and the son of Richard Jesse and Beatrice Lucy Harford of 21 Spanbourn Avenue.

Hayward Close - Cpl Edwin George Hayward of the 7th Battalion Kings Shropshire Light Infantry died aged 23 on 2 August 1917 in Tilloy, France. Edwin was from Shropshire, but his parents were residents of Chippenham, residing in Ashfield Road. He enlisted in the early months of the war and served for 18 months on active service, surviving many close calls.

Tanner Close - Frederick Thomas Tanner was a Private in the 2nd Wiltshire Regiment. He was one of five sons of John and Elizabeth Tanner, who lived at 10 'The Gardens' Ladds Lane, that served in the Army. Frederick lived in Pietermaritzburg, Natal with his wife Elizabeth. He tragically died on the Somme on 18 October 1916 aged 28 and is buried at Warlencourt British cemetery.

Keen artist, angler and dental apprentice Herbert Arthur Tanner was a Private in 'D' Squadron of the Royal Wiltshire Hussars. Born in Chippenham, he lived with his Mother Ruth at 73 Wood Lane. Whilst serving in Rouen, he was kicked by a horse and died on 14 August 1916.

The next group of streets off Webbington Road were built c1992.

Chivers Road - Albert Edward Chivers was a Private in the 11th Essex Regiment. On the 28 May 1918 at the age of 19, he was declared missing presumed dead and is commemorated on the Tyne Cot memorial in Belgium. Albert was the son of George and Rosanna Chivers of 1 St Mary Street, the third they had lost in the war. Albert was a member of Chippenham Amateur Swimming Club and played for Chippenham Cricket Club. Albert's brothers who also died in the First World War were; Sgt Edwin George Chivers of the 5th Wiltshire Regiment died of wounds in Mesopotamia aged 25 on 10 April 1916 and Private Sydney James Chivers of the 2nd Wiltshire Regiment was killed at Ypres on 24 October 1914.

Also, Michael John Chivers died on 27 August 1943 whilst serving with the Royal Navy, during the Second World War. He was a Stoker 1st Class on HMS Egret, which was the first Allied warship to be sunk with a guided missile. The HMS Egret was hunting U-boats off the coast of Portugal when it came under attack from a squadron of Dornier aircraft. 194 crew were lost, including 4 from the RAF Signals. Michael was the son of Michael and Phoebe Chivers, and lived in Hardenhuish with his wife Ruby Joan Chivers.

Massey Close - Private Albert Frederick Massey of the 1st Norfolk Regiment was born in London and was the husband of Winnie Ethel Massey, of 31 Loyalty Street. Albert died serving in Holland aged 32 on 6 April 1945.

Rowe Mead - Simeon Rowe was born in Fowey in Cornwall, but was a resident of Chippenham, working at the Capital and Counties Bank in the High Street. He was also the Honorary Secretary of Chippenham Amateur Swimming Club. Simeon served in the 26th Battalion Royal Fusiliers, known as the 'Bankers Battalion'. He was killed in action during a midnight attack on 14 December 1916, and is buried at Ridgewood cemetery in Belgium. His parents, Mr and Mrs Rowe of Fowey, had four other sons involved in the war, and at the time of Simeon's death aged 23, one was a prisoner, one wounded and in hospital, one serving in the Royal Navy and another as a munitions worker.

Leading Aircraftsman Christopher Rumble died due to the result of an airplane crash in Cornwall, during the Second World War.

Rumble Dene - Leading Aircraftsman Christopher Hubert Rumble served with the 179 Squadron RAF Volunteer Reserve. In 1944 he was based at RAF St Eval in Cornwall on Air Sea Rescue duties. On 31 December 1944 the Vickers Warwick aircraft he was flying in crashed at Trewollvas Farm, St Colomb Major. Christopher and five other men perished in the incident, he was only 20 years old. The son of Frank and Rosa Rumble of Chippenham, he was brought back to his home town, and buried in London Road cemetery.

Swayne Close - Arthur Henry Swayne was a Private in the 24th (Works) Battalion of the Labour Corps. Born in Chippenham, he was the son of William and Emily Swayne of 17 Springfield Buildings and a Blacksmith by trade. He died after the end of the First World War on 24 January 1919 aged 39, probably of injuries sustained or through illness. He is buried at Duisans British cemetery in Etrun, France.

Webb Close - William Webb lived with his wife Alice Webb at 6 Ladds Lane. He served as a Private in the 9th Battalion Northamptonshire Regiment. William died on 23 November 1918 aged 47 and is buried in Thetford cemetery.

James Webb was a Lance Corporal in the 1st Battalion Wiltshire Regiment. He was born in Atworth but lived with his wife Norah at Meadowfield, Frogwell. He was killed in action aged 29 on 28 August 1914 at Mons and is remembered on a memorial plaque in Atworth Church. He was not on record with the CWGC until 2008, therefore not actually on the Town memorial, but fully deserves to be mentioned.

Off Danes Close;

Dummer Way - Alfred James Dummer was the son of James and Isabella Dummer of Hawthorne Road and was an employee of Westinghouse. He served as a Private in the 4th Dorset Regiment and died aged 27 at Normandy on 15 July 1944.

Hancock Close - Walter Hancock was a Lance Corporal in the 2nd Battalion Wiltshire Regiment. He was killed in action aged 23 on 24 October 1914 at Ypres in Belgium. His parents were Jacob and Mary Hancock of 7 Factory Lane. Walter is commemorated on the Congregational Church Memorial.

Ladas Harcourt Hancock was a Gunner in the 60th Howitzer Battery Royal Field Artillery. He lived at Crossbrook(e) Cottages 227 London Road. Before the war, Ladas worked as an Auxiliary Postman. He was already serving when war was declared, and was only 18 on enlistment in 1912. He served in France before moving to Mesopotamia, and it was close to the Tigris river that Ladas succumbed to his wounds at the aged of 21 on 18 April 1916. Tragically, he was one of four members of his Wesleyan Sunday school class who died in the war, only one returning home.
His unusual first name is explained by his year of birth; Ladas was the name of the horse that won the Derby in 1894!

Off King Henry Drive;

Hatherell Road - Private Henry John Hatherell of 9 Lowden Hill joined the 6th Battalion Wiltshire Regiment as a Bugler at the age of 16. Henry was the son of John William and Emily Eliza Hatherell. He was a former employee of Chippenham Signal works and pupil of Ivy Lane school. He died on 4 July 1917 of his wounds at Boulogne aged only 19.

Private William James Hatherell lived at 1 Cowleaze Terrace, 38 Sheldon Road. William was part of the 11th Battalion Somerset Light Infantry and died aged 39 on 6 November 1918. He accidentally drowned whilst crossing the river Scheldt in Belgium and is buried in Pecq.

Penny Lane - Sidney Alan Penny was a Corporal in the 1st Battalion Wiltshire Regiment. He was a resident of Chippenham when the war started, and was tragically killed in action at Neuve Chappelle on 24 October 1914

Pinfield Lane - Frederick Bertram Pinfield was a Lance Corporal in the 13th Battalion Kings Royal Rifle Corps. He went missing at Passchendaele on 29 September 1917, aged 36. He is commemorated on the Tyne Cot memorial in Belgium. Frederick lived at 17 Audley Road with his wife Rosa and was the son of Mr and Mrs HG Pinfield of 44 Park Lane. He was very active in the local sports scene playing cricket and football, whilst his father was chairman of the Wiltshire Football league.

Off Webbington Road are;

Morse Close - Henry George Morse was the son of Lucy Hemmings of 10 Timber Street and William Morse. He was serving as a Stoker First Class on the HMS Lassoo, in the North Sea, when it was sunk by a sea mine on 13 August 1916. Henry died at sea aged 22.

Sidney Ivor Morse was the son of Arthur and Diana Morse of 25 The Causeway. A Private in the 1st Battalion Wiltshire Regiment, Sidney was 'killed instantaneously by a German bullet' at Ypres on 2 February 1915. He was described as a 'good soldier and always cheerful'.[385]

Payne Close - Arthur John Payne was a Private in the 5th Battalion Wiltshire Regiment. He was born in Walcot, Bath and was the son of Alfred Henry and Harriet Mary Payne of 27 Park Lane. Arthur was

---

[385] Wiltshire Times, 20 March 1915.

killed in action aged only 19 on 29 March 1917, whilst serving on the Nahrwan Canal in Iraq.

Herbert Henry Payne was a Private in the 1st Battalion Devonshire Regiment, and died on 17 April 1917 at the Western Front. Herbert was born in Frome, but he and his wife Sarah, lived at 18 St Mary Street.

Stapleford Close - Frank Stapleford was a Private in the 2nd Battalion Wiltshire Regiment. He was a resident of Bath, but he was born in Calne and his parents George and Elizabeth Stapleford lived at Derry Hill. Frank was killed in action at Festubert in France on 15 June 1915.

Tavinor Drive - Arthur Herbert George Tavinor was a Private in the 7th Battalion Queen's Own Royal West Kent Regiment. Arthur was born in Chippenham and was the son of Mr and Mrs George Tanner of 62 Marshfield Road. He was declared missing presumed dead aged only 19 on 8 August 1918.

Another group off Canal Road are;

Dickson Way - 2nd Lieutenant William Herbert Dickson served with the 2nd/4th Loyal North Lancashire Regiment. He was originally from Preston but moved to Chippenham to work as a solicitor. He died on the 8 June 1917 in Ypres, Belgium.

Leopold Jordan. Photograph - Larry Salmon (Great Nephew).

Jordan Close - Leopold John Jordan was a Company Quartermaster Sergeant in the 6th Wiltshire Regiment. Born in Somerset, Leopold later lived with his mother at 2 Park Lane whilst working as a clerk for Smith & Marshall Solicitors. He was a member of the Constitutional Club Shooting team, the local operatic society and St Andrews Choir. His father was Headmaster of Christian Malford School. He was listed as 'missing presumed dead' on 4 November 1916 whilst in action on the Somme.

Wicks Drive - Henry John Wicks was a Private in the 14th Battalion Royal Warwickshire Regiment. He was born in Chippenham and lived with his parents Henry John and Mary Ann Wicks at 36 St Mary Street. He died of wounds received on the Somme on 30 July 1916.

Wishart Way - John Waddie Wishart was a Private in the 15th Battalion Welsh Borders Regiment. He was born in St Paul's, Bristol and later lived at 5 Timber Street with his wife Emily Louise Wishart. He was declared 'missing presumed dead' at Neuve Chappelle on 7 January 1915.

Our final street name is another in honour of a Chippenham serviceman who died, but this time it is actually in France. Pilot Officer Thomas Humphrey Borg-Banks died on 16 May 1940 aged 19, after the Westland Lysander he was flying was shot down whilst in combat against ten German aircraft.
A former London Road resident, Thomas joined the RAF in 1938 aged 17, and at the time of his death was a member of the RAF's 13 Squadron. His plane came down near the small French town of Vieux Conde, which is close to the border with Belgium. **Rue des Anglais** in Vieux Conde was named in honour of Thomas and his rear gunner who had also died in the crash.[386]

---

[386] Western Daily Press, 24th August 1946.

Conclusion

Street names are an important source of local history. For a new resident they can be a first clue to the history of their new home, and potentially spark an interest in the history of their surroundings. Street names can act as a memorial to local worthies. They are also an opportunity not to be wasted. Developers keen on thematic names for selling purposes should not overlook their obligation to carefully choose names. Equally, local authorities must challenge, or advise of more appropriate names when necessary, calling on the advice of historians and consulting public records as required. A developer who does this shows consideration of the impact of their project which will go some way to appease local objections to the build that, once started, will remain.
Chippenham will inevitably grow in size and as it does the past should not be forgotten.
Chippenham has lost its bridge, but it still has its river. Lots of unique buildings were demolished rather than restored, but there are many fine examples that still survive.
Local pride can be bolstered through commemoration of the past. We must encourage the next generation to care about their local community and feel empowered to stand up and oppose permanent destruction of local assets such as those that took place after the Second World War and in some cases continue today. A balance needs to be found between future needs and our heritage, otherwise Chippenham will lose its identity and become a 'commuter town' like any other.

Acknowledgements

The following people have helped me in some way to make this book happen. Many people have been kind enough to allow use of photographs from their personal collections. These have been credited in the captions underneath them rather than here. Other contributions are referenced using the numbered 'in-text' footnotes.

Ray Alder, Ann Brinkworth and the Friends of Chippenham Museum.
Melissa Barnett and the staff of Chippenham Museum.
John Belcher
Cam Blake
Ian & Louise Dallimore
Melissa Dallimore
Emily Meehan
Nick Selby
Wiltshire and Swindon History Centre.

Bibliography

Alder, R., (2011), *Chippenham and the Wilts & Berks Canal*, Hobnob Press.

Baines, Richard, (2009), *A History of Chippenham from Alfred to Brunel*, Hobnob Press.

Barrett, G., & Jefferies, S., (1985), *100 Pictures of Chippenham Past*, Chippenham Civic Society.

Behe, G., (2012), On Board RMS Titanic: Memories of the Maiden Voyage, The History Press.

Chamberlain, Joseph A., (1976), *Chippenham: Some Notes on its History*, Chippenham Charter Trustees, Chippenham.

Clements, Eric L., (2016), *Captain of the Carpathia: The Seafaring Life of Titanic Hero Sir Arthur Henry Rostron*, Bloomsbury.

Coggles, J. & N., (1998), *The History of St Mary's Parish, Chippenham, 1855-1998*, St Mary's Roman Catholic Church.

Crick, Julia & Van Houts, Elisabeth, (2011), *A Social History of England, 900-1200*, Cambridge University Press.

Cruickshanks, E., Handley, S., & Hayton, D., (eds), (2002), *The History of Parliament: The House of Commons 1690-1715*, Boydell & Brewer.

Daniell, J.J, (1870), *Chippenham, and the neighbourhood, during the Great Rebellion*.

Daniell, J.J., (1894), *The History of Chippenham*, Houlston.

Endacott, F.J., (1978), *Westmead Junior School, Chippenham 1858-1978: A Brief History*, Unknown publisher.

Goldney, F.H., (1889), *Records of Chippenham relating to the Borough, from 1554 to 1889*, Unknown publisher.

Gover, J.E.B., (1939), *The Place-Names of Wiltshire*, Cambridge University Press

Grice, F., (1977) *Who's who in Kilverts*, The Kilverts Society.

Griffiths, T.J., (1982), *Chippenham Tour 1982*, Unknown publisher.

Henson, B., (1982), *Pew Hill House, Chippenham: A Brief History*, B Henson.

Jackson, J.E., (1856), *On the History of Chippenham*, Unknown Publisher.

Jackson, J.E., (1869), Chippenham; Notes of its History. Read at the General Meeting of the Wiltshire Archaeological Society, Unknown publisher.

Jefferies, S., (1987), *A Chippenham Collection*, Chippenham Civic Society, Chippenham.

Leleux, S., (1965), *Brotherhoods, Engineers,* David & Charles.

Marshall, R., (2005), *Chippenham Memories*, Tempus.

Perkins, John, (1905), *A History of the Borough of Chippenham*, Chippenham.

Pevsner, N., (1975), *The Buildings of England - Wiltshire.*

Platts, Arnold, (1947), *A History of Chippenham - AD 853-1946*, Wiltshire Gazette, Devizes.

Platts, Arnold, (1957), *The story of St Pauls County School: A centenary year, 1857-1957*, Unknown publisher.

Smith, C., (1977), *Chippenham Walkabout*, Chippenham Civic Society.

Tanner, G., (1972), *The Calne Branch*, Oxford Publushing Company.

Taylor, K. S., (2012), *Dry Shod to Chippenham: A History of Maud Heath's Ancient Causeway*, Ex-Libris Press.

Taylor, K. S., (2015), *From Domesday to Demolition: A History of the Flour Mill in Chippenham, Wiltshire 1086-1957*, Ex-Libris Press.

Twydell, D., (1986), *Defunct F.C*, Unknown publisher.

White, George A.H., (1924), *Chippenham in Bygone days*, George Simpson & Co, Devizes.

100 not out!: Chippenham Methodist Church, Chippenham 1909-2009, Chippenham Central Methodist Church.

Websites

www.bbc.co.uk/history/domesday/

www.britishnewspaperarchive.co.uk

www.cwgc.org

www.pro-patria.co.uk

http://www.workhouses.org.uk/Chippenham/